To Our Readers

Every day, there are times when you want to know more about something. It may be about how plants grow, or how electric motors work. You may want a certain fact about Abraham Lincoln, earth satellites, Bolivia, the invention of the piano, or what causes colds —to take just a few examples. Sometimes you need more information than a teacher, your parents, or a schoolbook can give. That's the time to turn to your GOLDEN BOOK ENCYCLOPEDIA.

This encyclopedia *is* for you. It has been made especially for readers who are starting to look up information on their own, and who want that information on their own bookshelf.

Into this encyclopedia have been put the most important facts of modern knowledge. The thousands of articles and color pictures, charts, diagrams, and maps make all this knowledge clear and exciting. Here is an endless parade of fascinating facts—facts you can depend upon for up-to-dateness and accuracy, because world-famous experts have checked them. Get into the habit of looking things up in your GOLDEN BOOK ENCYCLOPEDIA. Use it to discover more about interesting subjects mentioned in school. Let it be your partner in homework and school projects.

Watch newspapers and television for important news about science and government, foreign countries, famous people, sports, plants and animals, literature and art, weather and exploration. Look up these subjects in the index of your GOLDEN BOOK ENCYCLOPEDIA. Then read about them.

In the evening, or on a rainy day, pick up any volume of your GOLDEN BOOK ENCYCLOPEDIA. Open it anywhere and start reading. Notice how interesting just about any subject can be when it is clearly explained and well pictured. You will find yourself getting interested in more and more kinds of information.

THE GOLDEN BOOK ENCYCLOPEDIA is your guide to knowledge. The more you read it, the better you will like it.

THE EDITORS

THE
GOLDEN BOOK
ENCYCLOPEDIA

VOLUME V—DAGUERREOTYPE TO EPIPHYTE

In Sixteen Accurate, Fact-filled Volumes Dramatically Illustrated
with More Than 6,000 Color Pictures

THE ONLY ENCYCLOPEDIA FOR YOUNG GRADE-SCHOOL CHILDREN

ACCURATE AND AUTHORITATIVE

ENTERTAININGLY WRITTEN AND ILLUSTRATED TO
MAKE LEARNING AN ADVENTURE

by Bertha Morris Parker

Formerly of the Laboratory Schools, University of Chicago
Research Associate, Chicago Natural History Museum

GOLDEN PRESS · NEW YORK

CONTRIBUTORS AND CONSULTANTS

HALL BARTLETT, Ed.D., Citizenship Education Project, Teachers College, Columbia University; Author

WALT DISNEY, Motion Picture and Television Producer

EVELYN MILLIS DUVALL, Ph.D., Author and Consultant on Family Life; Authority on Child Development

EDNA E. EISEN, Ph.D., Professor of Geography, Kent State University

J. ALLEN HYNEK, Ph.D., Associate Director, Smithsonian Astrophysical Observatory

LELAND B. JACOBS, Ph.D., Professor of Education, Teachers College, Columbia University

ELEANOR M. JOHNSON, M.A., Director of Elementary School Services, Graduate Division, Wesleyan University

HERBERT A. LANDRY, M.S., Ph.D., Director, Bureau of Educational Program Research and Statistics, New York City Public Schools

MILTON LEVINE, M.D., Associate Professor of Pediatrics, New York Hospital

WILLY LEY, Professor of Science, Fairleigh Dickinson University; Rocket Expert and Author

NORMAN LLOYD, M.A., Teacher of Literature and Materials of Music, Juilliard School of Music

LENOX R. LOHR, M.E., D.Eng., D.Sc., President, Museum of Science and Industry, Chicago

WILL C. MCKERN, D.S., Former Director, Milwaukee Public Museum; Anthropologist

RICHARD A. MARTIN, B.S., Curator, N. W. Harris Public School Extension, Chicago Natural History Museum

MAURICE PATE, Executive Director, United Nations Children's Fund (UNICEF)

NORMAN VINCENT PEALE, D.D., LL.D., Litt.D., LH.D.; Minister, Marble Collegiate Church, New York; Author

RUTHERFORD PLATT, B.A., Member of Two North Pole Expeditions with Admiral MacMillan; Author of Nature Books

ILLA PODENDORF, M.S., Teacher of Science, University of Chicago Laboratory Schools; Author of Science Books

MARY M. REED, Ph.D., Supervisor of Little Golden Books; Formerly of Teachers College, Columbia University

JOHN R. SAUNDERS, M.A., Chairman, Department of Public Instruction, American Museum of Natural History

GLENN T. SEABORG, Ph.D., LL.D., D.Sc., Chancellor and Professor of Chemistry, University of California, Berkeley; Associate Director, University of California Radiation Laboratory; Co-winner of Nobel Prize for Chemistry, 1951

LOUIS SHORES, Ph.D., Dean of the Library School, Florida State University; Author and Authority on Reference Materials

NILA BANTON SMITH, Ph.B., Ph.D., Professor of Education and Director of The Reading Institute, New York University

BRYAN SWAN, M.S., Teacher of Physical Science, University of Chicago Laboratory Schools; Author

SAMUEL TERRIEN, S.T.M.; Th.D., Auburn Professor of the Old Testament, Union Theological Seminary

JESSIE TODD, M.A., Formerly of the Art Department, University of Chicago; Art Lecturer; Contributor to Art Magazines

LLOYD B. URDAL, Ph.D., Assistant Professor, School of Education, State College of Washington

JANE WERNER WATSON, B.A., Editor and Author of More Than a Hundred Golden Books

WILLIAM S. WEICHERT, M.S., Supervisor of Science, Oakland (Calif.) Public Schools

PAUL A. WITTY, Ph.D., Professor of Education, Northwestern University; Specialist on Gifted Children

STAFF

ROBERT D. BEZUCHA, Project Director; NORMAN F. GUESS, Editorial Director; R. JAMES ERTEL, Managing Editor; PAULINE NORTON, Assistant Project Director; ALICE F. MARTIN, Associate Editor. Staff Editors: GENEVIEVE CURLEY, JOAN FALK, HESTER GELB, RICHARD D. HARKINS.

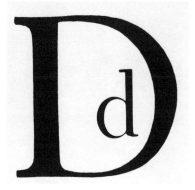

The letter *D* was probably in the beginning a picture of a door (⊓). The Phoenicians drew it in different ways (◁△▷). The Greeks wrote it as a simple triangle (△). It is still written in this way in modern Greek. The Romans changed it to this: D. It came down to the English alphabet from the Romans without change.

D is not always sounded the same way. It has different sounds in *day*, *talked*, and *soldier*. In such words as *handkerchief* and *handsome* it is silent.

DAGUERREOTYPE (da GER o type) George Washington never had his picture taken. He had it painted many times, but he lived before the days of photographs.

The daguerreotype was an early kind of photograph. Instead of a film or a glass plate, a sheet of copper was used. It was coated with a mixture of chemicals just as films and plates are now.

The name "daguerreotype" comes from the name of the Frenchman who invented it. He was Louis Daguerre, who was born the year Washington became president.

Daguerreotypes were not very good pictures. People soon found ways of improving on them. We owe the beautiful photographs we have now partly to Daguerre. (See INVENTIONS; PHOTOGRAPHY.)

It sometimes took 30 minutes to take a picture in the early days of daguerreotypes.

Cheese

BUTTER

Electric Milker

Milk

DAIRYING In different parts of the world different animals are valued for the milk they give. The goat, camel, llama, reindeer, yak, sheep, and water buffalo are among them. But in the world as a whole by far the most important milk producer is the cow. Caring for cows and the milk they produce is called dairy farming, or dairying. Cows raised especially for their milk are called dairy cows.

We have dairying to thank not only for milk itself, but also for cream, cheese, butter, and ice cream. It is hard to imagine how much milk the people of a big country need. The people of the United States eat or drink more than 55 billion pounds of milk and milk products every year.

The picture at the top of the next page shows a dairy farm. The big building in the picture is a barn where the cows stay when they are not out on pasture. The milking is done there. A modern barn like this one is big and airy. The second floor is a hayloft. The tall round buildings are silos. Here chopped green cornstalks and

Dairy farms are found in every state in the United States.

other such plant food are stored for the cows to eat in winter.

Dairy farming means much hard work. The cows and the barns must be kept very clean. The cows must be milked twice every day. The milk must be strained, cooled, and rushed to a dairy. The silos must be filled, and crops must be planted.

Machines make dairying easier than it used to be. On a dairy farm there are likely

nary dairy cow gives only a few quarts of milk a day. But the very best milkers give more than 50 quarts a day. The record is held by a Holstein cow. It is easy to see that the amount of milk a cow gives means a great deal to a dairy farmer. The amount of cream in the milk is important, too. Some kinds of cows—Jerseys, for instance —give milk that is especially rich in cream. (See BUTTER; CATTLE; MILK.)

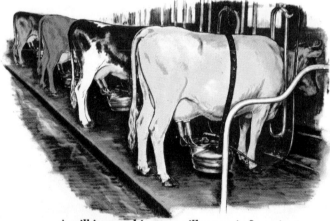

A milking machine can milk a cow in five minutes.

Milk trucks are like big thermos bottles.

to be milking machines, milk and cream separators, milk coolers, farm machinery for helping raise food for the cows, and trucks to carry the milk to the dairy.

The pastures on a dairy farm are important. The best dairy farms are in regions where there is good pasture grass. Wisconsin and New York are famous for such farms. In Europe, the Netherlands and Denmark are famous for dairy lands.

Dairy cattle have been greatly improved. Records are kept at big dairy farms of the amount of milk each cow gives. An ordi-

Milk is tested for purity and richness.

The old section of Damascus has open markets.

DAMASCUS The city of Damascus is in Syria, one of the countries that, with Egypt, make up the United Arab Republic. Damascus is a very old city, one of the oldest in the world. We know that it is at least 4,000 years old, and it may be much older.

Damascus is in an oasis in the Syrian Desert. A river from mountains near by brings water to it. It has such beautiful gardens that it has been called the "Pearl of the Desert."

Over the centuries Damascus has been a center of trade and travel. Today's cars and buses follow ancient caravan routes through it. Many of its streets are lined with bazaars. One of these streets is "The Street Called Straight." For a mile and a half it has a roof over it. Damascus has one of the world's most famous mosques.

Fifteen hundred years ago Damascus was famous for its steel. The ironworkers of Damascus may have been the first people to make true steel. A sword made of the best Damascus steel was strong enough to cut through a rod of iron and sharp enough to cut through a flimsy silk scarf floating in the air.

Once during the Crusades, according to an old story, Richard the Lionhearted was boasting about his sword to Saladin, the ruler of the Moslems. To prove how strong it was, he cut an iron rod in two with it. Then Saladin handed Richard a soft silk pillow and asked him to try his sword on it. Richard could not cut it. Saladin with his sword of Damascus steel then cut it in two with one stroke. (See IRON AND STEEL.)

DAMOCLES More than 2,000 years ago Dionysius the Elder was the ruler of the old Greek city of Syracuse. Damocles was a member of his court.

Damocles talked a great deal about how lucky Dionysius (dy o NISH i us) was to be a ruler. At last Dionysius grew tired of hearing about his good fortune. He decided he would teach Damocles a lesson.

Dionysius planned a royal banquet and gave Damocles the seat of honor. Damocles felt very well pleased with himself. But in the middle of the meal he happened to look up. Just above his head a very sharp sword hung by a single hair. If the hair should break, Damocles would be killed. He did not enjoy the rest of the dinner.

Dionysius, of course, had ordered the sword hung above Damocles' head. He wanted Damocles to know that a ruler's life is not easy—that often his life is in danger. Today someone may say that the sword of Damocles is hanging over his head. He means that, because of his position, he fears misfortune ahead.

A sword hung by a hair over Damocles' head.

DAMON AND PYTHIAS Many centuries ago two friends, Damon and Pythias, lived near the Greek city of Syracuse. Dionysius, the ruler of Syracuse, accused Pythias of plotting against him. He ordered Pythias put to death.

Pythias begged for time to visit his wife and children. Damon offered to take Pythias' place in prison. Damon promised that if Pythias did not return he would die instead. Dionysius agreed to the plan, and Damon entered the prison.

Pythias did not return on time, and it seemed that Damon would die. But at the very last moment, Pythias rushed into the prison. His horse had been hurt on the way, and he had run a long distance to save Damon's life.

Still Damon offered to die for his friend. Pythias refused to let him. When Dionysius heard each offering to give up his life for the other, he ordered that the lives of both be spared. He did not wish to separate such loyal friends. Ever since that time the names of Damon and Pythias have stood for true friendship.

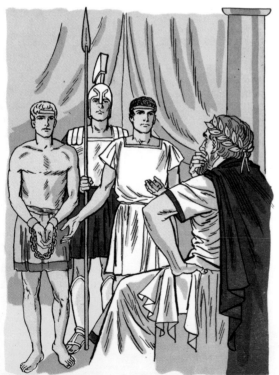

Damon and Pythias each offered to die for the other.

DAMS A dam is a wall across a stream. It holds back the water of the stream. It may make it spread out to form a big lake.

It sounds much easier to build a wall across a stream than it is. Water is heavy. A tin can a foot wide, a foot long, and a foot deep would hold just a cubic foot of water. A cubic foot of water weighs about 62½ pounds. If the lid of such a can were lying at the bottom of a river 20 feet deep, and that is not at all deep for a river, the water on top of it would weigh more than half a ton. A dam to hold back a river has to be very strong. It has to be especially strong at the base, because there the pressure of the water it is holding back is greatest.

People were not the first engineers to build dams. Beavers built them long before men did. But men have been building dams for several thousand years. The ancient Egyptians built dams along the Nile. The Babylonians built dams along the Tigris.

Beavers build their dams of tree trunks and mud. The first dams men built were made of earth. Now most of them are made of concrete strengthened with steel.

Beavers need ponds to build their homes in. Their dams make the water of streams spread out to form ponds. People build dams for several reasons. They may dam a tiny stream flowing in a gully to keep the stream from making the gully wider and deeper and spoiling much good land. They

Hoover Dam is as high as a 60-story skyscraper.

may dam a bigger stream to hold back the water after heavy rains and prevent floods. They may build a big dam to make an artificial lake. The lake may furnish water for a city. It may furnish water for irrigation. At the same time it may provide miles of shore line, with chances for bathing and for boating.

Another reason for building dams is to keep the water in a river deep enough for boats to travel on the river. Still another is to make an artificial waterfall. The falling water may be used to turn mill wheels or big generators for generating currents of electricity. Many dams serve more than one purpose.

The highest dam in the world is Mauvoisin Dam in Switzerland. This dam is 777 feet high, about 50 feet higher than Hoover Dam, which is the highest dam in the United States. On each square foot at the base of Mauvoisin the water is pushing with a force of more than 20 tons.

One of the oldest concrete dams is the Aswan Dam across the Nile. It was built in 1902. Later it was made somewhat higher.

The biggest of all concrete dams is the Grand Coulee Dam. It dams the Columbia River. Enough concrete was used in this dam to build a four-lane highway all the way from Chicago to New Orleans. (See ELECTRICITY; IRRIGATION; WATER SUPPLY.)

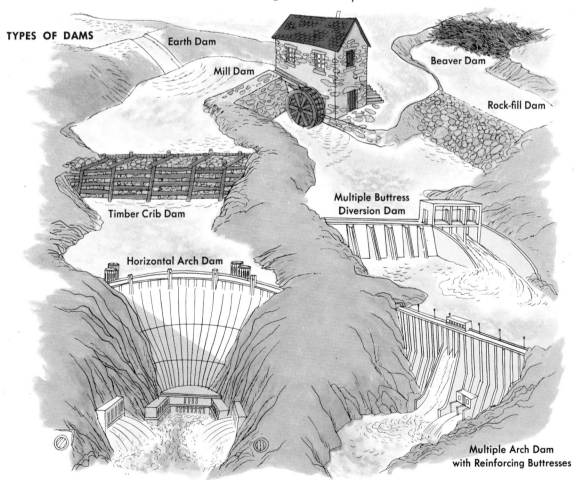

TYPES OF DAMS

Earth Dam

Mill Dam

Beaver Dam

Rock-fill Dam

Timber Crib Dam

Multiple Buttress Diversion Dam

Horizontal Arch Dam

Multiple Arch Dam with Reinforcing Buttresses

Indian Ceremonial Dancing

DANCING Long ago, so long ago that no one knows when it was, people began to dance to express some of their feelings. They danced to show that they were happy about a big harvest. They danced to celebrate a victory in war. They danced as a way of praying to their gods.

Today there is dancing of many different kinds. Much of it is just for fun. But some kinds of dancing are true art. Most dancing is done to music. But there can be dancing without music.

Folk dancing is usually done in groups. The people of many countries have their own folk dances. The square dances so many people enjoy are folk dances. Most folk dances are lively and gay.

In social dancing two people dance together. Social dancing is sometimes called ballroom dancing. The waltz used to be the most popular of the ballroom dances. Some of the pleasantest music we hear was written for waltzing.

Some dancing is done on the stage for other people to watch. This dancing takes much skill and practice. Tap dancing is this kind of dancing. So is acrobatic dancing of all kinds.

Ballet is dancing to watch, too. A good ballet dancer must begin to learn dancing when he is very young. A ballet tells a story without any words to help.

Many operas and musical shows use dances to help tell their stories. The costumes of the dancers are often beautiful.

Dancing still has a part in some religions, especially in religions of the Far East. Priestesses in these religions may spend most of their lives in perfecting their dancing. (See ARTS; BALLET; OPERA.)

DANUBE RIVER "The Beautiful Blue Danube" is the name of a famous waltz written by Johann Strauss, who lived in Vienna, a big city on the Danube River. The Danube is not really bluer than other rivers. But in many places it is beautiful. It is, moreover, one of the most important rivers in the world.

The Danube rises in the Black Forest in southern Germany. From there it flows southeast into the Black Sea. By air it is less than 1,000 miles from the place where the Danube rises to its mouth in the Black Sea. But the river wanders about so much that it is more than 1,700 miles long. Next to the Volga, it is the longest river in

TYPES OF DANCING

Hungarian Folk Dancing

Minuet Court Dancing

Ballet

Dervish Dancing

Spanish Fandango

Russian Folk Dancing

Ballroom Dancing

Interpretive Dancing

The Danube is an important shipping route.

Europe. More than 300 branches flow into it. A canal connects it to the Rhine River.

Eight different countries border the Danube. The capitals of three of them are on the river. One is Vienna, the capital of Austria. The second is Budapest, the capital of Hungary. The third is Belgrade, the capital of Yugoslavia.

In places the Danube flows sleepily across level farmland. In one spot it spreads out so that it is like a broad lake. Many farm villages are on its banks. In other places it rushes between steep cliffs. Old castles are perched on some of these cliffs. One gorge through which it passes in the mountains to the east of Belgrade is called the Iron Gate.

For hundreds of years the Danube has been a great highway. Armies have marched along its valley. Boats have carried goods up and down it. Before World War II the flags of a dozen countries could be seen flying from the boats on the river. Now travel along it is less free than it was then. (See AUSTRIA; BLACK SEA; BULGARIA; CZECHOSLOVAKIA; HUNGARY; RUMANIA; VIENNA; YUGOSLAVIA.)

DARDANELLES The Dardanelles is a narrow strait that joins the little Sea of Marmara to the Aegean Sea. It is about 40 miles long. At its narrowest place it is only about a mile wide.

The Dardanelles is one of the most important straits in the world. All the ships traveling between the Black Sea and the Mediterranean have to pass through it. The land on both sides of the strait belongs to Turkey. In a war Turkey could close the strait to the ships of any nation she pleased.

An old name for the Dardanelles is the Hellespont. There is an old Greek legend of two lovers who lived on opposite sides of the Hellespont. Their names were Hero and Leander. Every night Leander swam across the Hellespont to visit Hero. But one stormy night the lamp in Hero's tower window was blown out by the strong wind and Leander, having nothing to guide him, drowned. Hero was so brokenhearted that she killed herself by leaping from her tower into the sea. (See BLACK SEA; BOSPORUS; STRAITS; TURKEY.)

DARK AGES The time we call the Middle Ages lasted for 1,000 years. The first few hundred years of the Middle Ages, until about 800, are often called the Dark Ages.

The Dark Ages began with the fall of the Roman Empire in 476. For some time the empire had been growing weaker. Roman soldiers who were in the British Isles, northern Europe, and other faraway parts of the empire had been called back to protect Rome. Tribes of barbarians were pushing into the empire from the north and east. The barbarians proved too strong for the Romans. They swarmed over all of western Europe that had been ruled by Rome.

Each family provided its own food and clothing.

The barbarians were fierce, wild fighters. They plundered the palaces of the rulers of Rome. They let the famous roads that led to Rome fall into decay. The barbarians could not read or write and cared nothing at all for the learning that had come down from the ancient Egyptians and Babylonians and Greeks. Life in the lands they overran came to be not very much better than the life lived by the cave men in much earlier days. No wonder the time is called the Dark Ages.

At last, however, the barbarians began to settle down. Many of them became farmers. But much of Europe was covered by forests, roamed by bands of robbers. Towns were small and far apart. There was little trade between these small towns. Not many people felt safe outside them.

Farmers in the Dark Ages lived in crude cottages.

But all through the Dark Ages the Christian Church grew in strength. The monks in their monasteries kept alive the learning of earlier times. Without the Christian Church the Dark Ages would have been much darker than they were.

While Europe was in the Dark Ages, other parts of the world were moving forward. The Arabs, who spread from the Near East across Africa into Spain, and the Chinese were going far ahead of the people of Europe. Art and learning flourished also in the great Byzantine Empire to the east. The Dark Ages were dark chiefly for Europe. And even in Europe there were the beginnings of ideas about government and trade that at last let the people work their way out of the Dark Ages. (See CASTLES; KNIGHTHOOD; MIDDLE AGES; MONKS AND MONASTERIES; MOORS.)

Monks helped keep alive the learning of the past.

DARWIN, CHARLES (1809-1882) In 1831 Charles Darwin set sail from England on the "Beagle" for a five-year trip around the world. This trip is a very important one in the history of science, for it led Darwin to write one of the world's most famous books. The book is *The Origin of Species*. It gives Darwin's ideas of how all the plants and animals of today have come from the very simple plants and animals that first lived on the earth. The book stirred up great arguments.

Darwin had not planned to be a scientist. He studied to be a doctor and then to be a minister. But all the while he was interested in plants and animals. A friend who knew about Darwin's interest in nature invited him to take the trip on the "Beagle."

On the voyage Darwin spent some time on the Galápagos Islands and became interested in the huge turtles there. He also visited Australia, Tasmania, and New Zealand. There he saw many strange plants and animals. Darwin was seasick for much of the voyage, but he came back with the notes for his great book.

These were Darwin's chief ideas: Many more plants and animals are produced than can possibly live. No two plants and animals, even of the same kind, are exactly alike. A young plant or animal may be different enough from its neighbors of the same kind to make it better fitted than the others for living where it does. In the struggle to live, this plant or animal is the one most likely to survive. Its offspring inherit the difference. Some of them, in turn, may change, too, in ways that make them still better fitted for living where they do. Finally, as the centuries go by, the plant or animal may be so different from its ancestors that it rates as a new kind, or species.

After his return to England, Darwin married his cousin, Emma Wedgwood. Together they had enough money so that Darwin did not have to work to earn a salary. He could spend all his time studying and writing about his beliefs.

The idea that all the plants and animals of today came from the simple plants and animals of long ago is called the "theory of evolution." Darwin's work did a great deal to bring scientists to believe in the theory. (See EVOLUTION.)

Darwin's voyage gave him a chance to study plants and animals all over the world.

Date Palm

Dried Dates

DATES For thousands of years dates have been one of the chief foods of the people in the dry lands near the Mediterranean Sea. They are the fruit of palm trees like those in the pictures.

The people in the lands where date palms grow say that these trees must keep their feet wet and their heads dry. The trees need water but they have to have bright sunshine, too. They grow well in the irrigated lands near the Tigris and Euphrates rivers. Dates are the chief crop in the oases of the Sahara. And millions of date palms grow along the Nile in Egypt.

From these hot, dry regions near the Mediterranean the date palm has been carried to other regions. There are date orchards in California and Arizona.

Date palms produce one crop a year. A healthy tree bears several clusters. A big cluster may weigh as much as 40 pounds. Dates are red or yellow before they are ripe. Ripe dates are purple.

When a tree is young, its dates are easy to gather. But as it gets older it grows tall. Gathering the dates from a palm 100 feet tall is not easy.

Many date palms grow in oases in the Sahara Desert.

Not all date palms bear dates. Some—the male trees—furnish only pollen. The ones that bear the dates are the female trees. Before dates will form, pollen from the flowers of the male trees must reach the flowers of the female trees. In the beginning date palms had to depend on the wind to carry their pollen. But long ago date growers found a way of making sure that pollen would reach the flowers of the female tree. They gathered bunches of pollen-bearing flowers and tied them to the clusters of flowers of the female tree.

Dates can be dried easily. They keep very well. Many people have never seen fresh dates. But dried dates are in the markets almost everywhere. (See POLLINATION.)

Incas measured years with a shadow pillar.

DATES Each year has a number. To tell the date of a happening, we give the number of the year. We say, for instance, that Columbus discovered America in 1492.

The years are numbered from the year that was supposed to be the one in which Christ was born. To give the date of earlier happenings, we count back from the year 1. We then put B.C. after the number. "B.C." stands for "before Christ." The dates of happenings after the birth of Christ sometimes have A.D. before the number. The initials "A.D." stand for the Latin words *anno Domini*. These words mean "in the year of our Lord."

Shadows marked dates at Stonehenge.

A.D. 1 was not actually the year when Christ was born. A mistake was made. Christ was born at least four years earlier. But when the mistake was discovered, it was too late to change the calendar.

Our way of numbering years did not begin till several hundred years after Christ died. Before then there were other ways of telling the date.

The Romans counted their years from the date of the founding of Rome. The Greeks counted their years from the date of the first Olympic games.

In still earlier times years were often named instead of numbered. Another plan was to number the years in a ruler's reign. In the Bible one date is "in the first year of Cyrus, king of Persia." "In the fourth year of Solomon's reign over Israel" is a Bible date, too. How well we would have to know lists of rulers if we now had dates like these! (See CALENDAR.)

The position of certain stars marks the Egyptians' year.

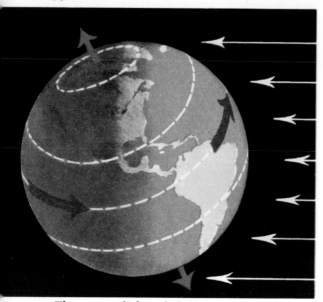

The sun can light only half the earth at one time.

DAY AND NIGHT The word "day" has two meanings. When we talk about the number of days in a year we are using "day" to mean 24 hours. But when we talk about day and night we are using "day" to mean the time between sunrise and sunset—the time when the sun is above the horizon.

Since the earth is shaped like a ball, the sun can shine on only half of it at a time. Always one half of the earth is having day and one half night. A place is moved from day into night and from night into day over and over by the spinning of the earth.

At the equator day and night are always the same length. They are each 12 hours long. The sun rises at 6 o'clock in the morning and sets at 6 o'clock in the evening.

On two days of each year—about March 20 and September 23—day and night are the same length all over the earth. Day and night would always be the same everywhere if it were not for the tilt of the earth as it spins around. For six months the North Pole is tilted toward the sun. In those months the northern hemisphere gets more hours of sunlight than the southern hemisphere. Days are longer than nights. South of the equator nights are longer than days.

For the other six months the North Pole is tilted away from the sun. Then the southern hemisphere gets more sunlight. Days are longer than nights. North of the equator nights are longer than days. Everywhere fall and winter are the seasons of long nights. Spring and summer are the seasons of long days.

Although during the spring and summer days are longer than nights, they are not all the same length. In New York, as all over the earth, the day is 12 hours long on the first day of spring. Days get longer and longer till June 21. On that date it is about 15 hours between sunrise and sunset. Then the days begin to get shorter.

The farther north one goes the longer the longest day is. North of the Arctic Circle, in "the land of the midnight sun," there are days or weeks or even months when the sun does not set at all. The North Pole has six months of continuous day.

Pictures of the midnight sun taken at intervals.

The fall and winter story is just the opposite of the spring and summer story. The North Pole in those months has continuous night. Of course, the sun is then shining on the South Pole 24 hours out of every 24.

On Christmas Day Quito, Ecuador, which is almost on the equator, has 12 hours of daylight. Melbourne, Australia, has 15. In Hammerfest, Norway, the sun does not rise at all during the day. On the Fourth of July the story—except for Quito—is very different. Melbourne has only 9 hours of daylight. Hammerfest has no night at all. (See CALENDAR; EARTH; SEASONS; TIME AND TIME TELLING.)

DAYS OF THE WEEK The seven days of the week are named in honor of the sun, the moon, and five of the planets. The five planets are Mercury, Venus, Mars, Jupiter, and Saturn. These were the only planets the people of long ago knew about. The sun, moon, and these five planets were supposed to take turns ruling over the days. The seven days from the sun's day to the sun's day became the week.

Sunday is the sun's day. Monday is the moon's day. Saturday is Saturn's day. Tuesday is Mars' day. Wednesday is Mercury's day. Thursday is Jupiter's day. And Friday is Venus' day. "Tuesday," "Wednesday," "Thursday," and "Friday" do not sound at all like "Mars' day," "Mercury's day," "Jupiter's day," and "Venus' day." The names of these four days came about in this way:

The planets were named for Roman gods and goddesses. Mars was the Roman god of war. Mercury was the messenger of the gods. Jupiter was the king of the gods. Venus was the goddess of beauty. The old Norse gods and goddesses were very much the same as the Roman ones. But they had different names. Our names Tuesday, Wednesday, Thursday, and Friday came from Norse gods. Tuesday is "Tiu's day," Wednesday is "Woden's day," Thursday is "Thor's day," and Friday is "Frigg's day."

We cannot change the number of days in a year without getting dates all out of place in the seasons. Our year is made for us by the journey of the earth around the sun. We cannot change the length of the day. The day is made for us by the turning of the earth on its axis. But there is no reason why we have to have seven days in a week. We could have any number of days we liked. Five-day, eight-day, and ten-day weeks have all been tried. If the people of long ago had known about Uranus, Neptune and Pluto, we might have ten days in a week instead of seven. But we are so used to seven now that few people would want to change. (See GREEK MYTHS; NORSE GODS AND GODDESSES.)

Sun
Sunday

Frigg
Friday

Woden
Wednesday

Thor
Thursday

Moon
Monday

Tiu
Tuesday

Saturn
Saturday

DEAD SEA The Dead Sea lies partly between Israel and Jordan. It is really a lake, not a sea. It is called a sea because its water is salty. In fact, its water is four or five times as salty as the water in the oceans of the world.

This lake is not as big as the Great Salt Lake in Utah. The Dead Sea is 47 miles long and 10 miles wide.

The Dead Sea lies in a deep valley far below the level of the oceans. The lake is 1,300 feet deep, but its surface is still nearly 1,300 feet below sea level.

The Jordan River brings water to the Dead Sea. No streams or rivers flow out of it. It does not get deeper because the water in it evaporates very fast. The climate is so hot and dry that the Dead Sea would get about 15 feet lower every year if no water were brought to it.

In ancient times travelers told many wild stories about the Dead Sea. There were, they said, never any waves on its surface. The air above it was so poisonous that it killed birds. And anyone who went near it was risking his life. Of course, these stories were not true.

The Dead Sea has stored up for thousands of years the minerals brought to it by the Jordan. Now many minerals besides salt can be got from its waters.

A "twenty-mule team" hauling borax in Death Valley.

DEATH VALLEY The floor of Death Valley is the lowest land in the Americas. It is 280 feet below sea level. This valley is in California near the Nevada border. There are ranges of mountains all around it. Death Valley, which is about 140 miles long, contains about two million acres of sun-baked, ghostly desert land.

The valley is one of the hottest places in the world. We think that a day when the temperature goes up to 100 degrees is very hot. In Death Valley the temperature sometimes goes above 130 degrees!

Death Valley is usually very dry. At times torrents of water rush down the Amargosa River into it. But as a rule the bed of the river is like a big, dry ditch.

Only the hardiest of desert plants and animals can live in Death Valley. There are some cactus and greasewood plants. There are a few desert rats, rattlesnakes, and horned toads. For the most part there is nothing but bare sand. In some places it has a coating of borax.

The valley got its name in 1849 when some of the people who were rushing to California to find gold died of thirst there. Now the valley has good roads and good hotels for winter tourists. But the tourists who visit it are glad that they do not have to stay there the year round.

MILES 0 10

Jordan River

DEAD SEA

Jericho

Jerusalem

J O R D A N

I S R A E L

DEAD SEA

Dead-Sea—1,292 feet below sea level

DECLARATION OF INDEPENDENCE

The United States of America really began on July 4, 1776. This was the day the Declaration of Independence was adopted by the 13 colonies.

For some time many people in the 13 colonies had wanted to break away from England. But no one colony was strong enough to stand alone. At last, in 1775, the leaders of the colonies called a meeting in Philadelphia. They formed the Continental Congress. In July of the next year they met again and decided to act together and declare their independence.

The Declaration of Independence told why the colonies wanted to be free. It listed the wrongs they had suffered. It went on to say that the colonies would now fight their own wars, make their own peace, carry on trade as they saw fit, and act in every way as an independent nation.

John Hancock was the president of the Continental Congress when the Declaration of Independence was adopted. Thomas Jefferson did most of the writing of it. He had the help, however, of such famous men as John Adams and Benjamin Franklin.

Fifty-six men signed the Declaration. As the last sentence of the Declaration says, these men by signing it pledged to one another "our lives, our fortunes, and our sacred honor." (See FOURTH OF JULY; JEFFERSON, THOMAS; LIBERTY BELL; PATRIOTS: U. S. HISTORY.)

Thomas Jefferson writing the Declaration.

U.S. Distinguished Flying Cross
U.S. Silver Star
U.S. Purple Heart
U.S. Congressional Medal of Honor
French Croix de Guerre
U.S. Navy Cross

DECORATIONS OF HONOR

We should be very proud of anyone we see wearing any of the medals in the picture. For these medals are given for great bravery in war. They are decorations of honor.

The oldest decoration of honor in the United States is the Purple Heart. George Washington founded it in 1782. The very highest decoration of the United States is the Congressional Medal of Honor. The picture shows three other decorations given to American heroes.

Other nations, too, give medals for bravery in war. Britain's highest decoration is the Victoria Cross. Many Canadian, as well as British, heroes wear it. The picture shows France's highest decoration. It is the Croix de Guerre—the "cross of war."

At important affairs abroad, many people wear wide ribbons, jeweled collars, or jeweled crosses. These decorations are much more showy than medals. They are signs that tell to what orders the wearers belong. Orders began back in the days of knighthood. They were groups of knights who had won fame by their deeds. England's Order of the Garter goes back 600 years. Its members wear a blue and gold ribbon garter. On it there is a motto in French which means, "Evil is he who thinks evil."

The Legion of Honor, founded by Napoleon, is one of the orders of France. One of Belgium's is the Order of the Elephant. There are many other such orders in European countries. Each one gives those that belong to it the privilege of wearing its badge—its decoration of honor.

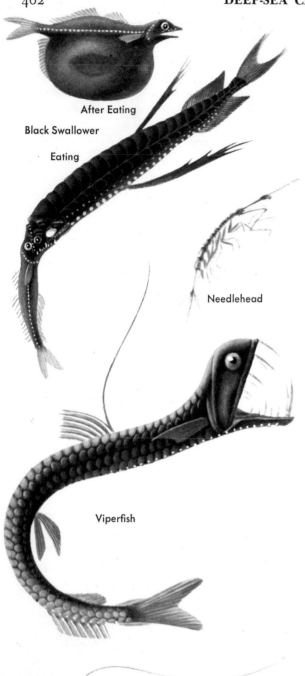

After Eating

Black Swallower

Eating

Needlehead

Viperfish

DEEP-SEA CREATURES

Most of the plants and animals that live in the ocean remain in the top 600-foot layer. Below this level conditions become less and less suitable for living things. At a depth of one mile the ocean is very cold and dark. No sunlight at all reaches down that far to give any light or heat. Plants cannot live there because without sunlight they cannot make food. Some animals, however, live in this dark, cold abyss.

Animals of the deep sea are strange-looking creatures. They look very different from their relatives in shallower waters. It is not surprising that they do, since they live under very different conditions. Their bodies fit these conditions.

Deep-sea creatures have thousands of pounds of water pressure on every square inch of their bodies. We do not feel the pressure of the air on our bodies because the pressure from the inside outward is as great as the pressure on the outside. Deep-sea animals are fitted to their environment in a similar way. The inside pressure is equal to the outside pressure.

When deep-sea animals are pulled up to the surface, they are likely to die at once. Not many of them can stand the sudden changes in temperature and pressure. A few kinds of fishes—those that have swim bladders—even turn inside out. They do so because at the surface the pressure inside their bodies is much greater than the pressure outside.

Most deep-sea animals are small. Any one that gets to be six feet long is a giant.

Shrimp

An animal as big as a man would have about six million pounds of pressure on its body at a depth of a mile. It is not surprising that most deep-sea creatures are small.

Many deep-sea fishes have enormous jaws, teeth, and eyes. The saber-toothed viperfish certainly has. The teeth of this fish are so long that it is difficult to see how it can ever close its mouth.

The viperfish often eats fish that are almost as large as itself. The black swallower can eat fish that are much bigger than it is. Its jaws and its stomach can stretch enormously.

Many animals of the deep sea eat other animals living there. Some live on the "rain" of dead plants and animals drifting down from surface waters.

Chemicals that glow in the dark are produced in the bodies of many deep-sea creatures. The angler has "lanterns" at the ends of stalks. The bathysphere fish has rows of pale-blue lights on its sides. And it has a red light and a blue one at the end of each of its two long tentacles. Both the teeth and the eyes of the viperfish glow in the deep-sea darkness with a weird light.

While many of the deep-sea fishes are ugly, others are beautiful. The five-lined constellation fish has a body which is flattened like that of a butterfly fish. Encircling the fish are glowing fringelike fins. On each side of its body there are five rows of gleaming lights.

The squids of the deep sea are beautiful creatures, too. Their long, graceful bodies are covered with organs that give off delicate red, blue, or green light. At the tip of each of a squid's two longest tentacles is a ball which glows with a reddish light.

Shrimp are very common in the deep sea. Organs inside their bodies make light-producing chemicals. These chemicals are dissolved in some of the water in their bodies. When the shrimp are in danger, this water pours out and forms glowing clouds. The light is believed to blind enemies and thus protect the shrimp by giving them a chance to escape.

Great numbers of very small animals swim or float about in the deep sea. Those that glow look to a deep-sea explorer like stars in a night sky. With its many-colored lights the "sky" of the deep sea must be as beautiful as the starry sky above us. But very few of us will ever see it. (See ADAPTATION TO ENVIRONMENT; FISHES.)

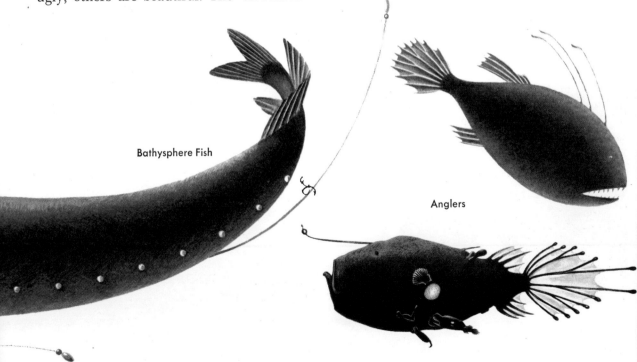

Bathysphere Fish

Anglers

DEEP-SEA EXPLORING Boys sometimes complain that all the world has been explored. There is, they say, no new place on the earth for explorers to go. But this idea is wrong. One part of the world is still largely unexplored. It is the deep sea.

There has been some deep-sea exploring. We know about some of the strange creatures of the deep sea. We know about the darkness and cold there.

The first deep-sea exploring was not to find out about the ocean itself but to recover sunken treasure. Many ships loaded with treasure have gone down to the bottom of the sea. Some treasure has been recovered, but a great deal still remains.

It is not easy to explore the deep sea. An undersea explorer has to have some way of breathing under water. Besides, he has to have some way of protecting himself from the terrific pressure of the water. We are used to having air press on our bodies. We do not even notice it. The pressure of the air is about 15 pounds on every square inch. Three thousand feet down in the ocean—a little more than half a mile—the pressure of the water is about 1,300 pounds on every square inch!

Diving suits furnished the first good way of exploring under water. One kind of diving suit is made mostly of rubber. The helmet is copper, with windows of glass. The shoes have heavy lead soles. Each shoe weighs nearly 20 pounds. Air is pumped down to the diver through a tube that leads into his helmet. Such a suit lets a diver go

Deep-sea Diver   Bathysphere

Many strange fishes live in the deep sea.

a few hundred feet down into the sea. But it is of no use for great depths. It could not stand the pressure.

With a metal diving suit an explorer can go down 700 feet. Such a suit can stand a pressure of 300 pounds a square inch. In 1932 a diver wearing a metal suit helped raise treasure worth $4,000,000 from the wreck of a sunken ship.

In 1927 William Beebe began making plans for going deeper into the sea than anyone had ever gone before. He was not hunting for treasure. He wanted to study the living things of the sea. Beebe decided that the best way to explore the sea would be in a hollow steel ball. A friend of his, Otis Barton, had such a ball built. Its walls were an inch and a quarter thick. It was only 4 feet 9 inches in diameter, but it weighed more than 5,000 pounds.

Beebe named the ball a "bathysphere." The first part of the word comes from Greek and means "deep." "Sphere" means "ball." The windows of the bathysphere could not be made of glass. No glass could stand the pressure. Quartz was used instead. The door into the bathysphere was only 14 inches across. The bathysphere had no air line. A tank of oxygen was carried inside. But there were electric light and telephone wires leading to the sphere.

Beebe and Barton made several exploring trips in the bathysphere. Once they went down 3,028 feet. They saw many creatures no one had ever seen before. Beebe wrote about their thrilling adventures in a book called *Half-Mile Down*.

Later Barton went down in another metal ball. He called it a "benthoscope." He reached a depth of 4,500 feet.

In February of 1954, another kind of diving vessel called a "bathyscaphe" went down 13,287 feet—a little over two and one-half miles. Perhaps the bathyscaphe and still newer diving vessels will help us discover more about the mysterious depths of the sea. (See ADAPTATION TO ENVIRONMENT; DEEP-SEA CREATURES.)

Robinson Crusoe was shipwrecked on an island.

DEFOE, DANIEL (1659-1731) While he was still in school in London, Daniel Defoe decided to be a writer. His early writings after he grew up were mostly pamphlets. One of his pamphlets displeased some men in the government, and Defoe was thrown into prison. As soon as he was freed, he went on with his writing.

He was 60 years old when he wrote the book which made him famous. It was called *The Life and Strange Surprising Adventures of Robinson Crusoe*. In those days it was considered a waste of time to read "made up" stories. Defoe based his book on the true story of Alexander Selkirk, a sailor who had been shipwrecked on a desert island. But Defoe made up most of the adventures of his hero. Readers thought the whole story was true.

Although Defoe wrote other books, none was as well liked as *Robinson Crusoe*. Boys and girls still read this story today. It has been translated into many languages.

He found the footprint in the sand.

PENNSYLVANIA

Elsmere

Site of Fort Christina (Swedish Settlement, 1638)

Wilmington

Newark

Cooch's Bridge
(Site of Delaware's
only Revolutionary
War Battle)

First State Capital
New Castle

Chesapeake and
Delaware Canal

Delaware River

D E L A W A R E

MARYLAND

Dover

F

DELAWARE

BAY

Milford

F

First Dutch Settlement in Delaware River Region, 1631 ▲ O Lewes

Nanticoke River

Seaford

Rehoboth
Bay

Laurel

Indian River
Bay

F

MARYLAND

DELAWARE The little state of Delaware is called the "First State" because it was the first of the original 13 states to join the Union. Its Old State House, built in 1792, stands in Dover, the state's capital. This state house is still used for state offices.

When a newly elected president of the United States is inaugurated, there is a parade in his honor. Of course, it is in Washington, D.C., the capital of the country. Representatives of the little first state always lead the parade.

No part of Delaware is far from the midpoint of the eastern coast of the United States. On the east, the state is bordered by the Delaware River, Delaware Bay, and the open Atlantic. It is in the northeastern part of a peninsula. West of the peninsula

Chemicals

Poultry

Garden Crops

F Fruit

Paper and Pulp

Textiles

Machinery

Dairying

Fish

Hardware

Shipping

▲ Historical Sites and Points of Interest

**ELEVATION
Feet**
0 – 300

Total state population 438,000
Area (square miles) 2,399

0   MILES   15

is Chesapeake Bay. The small state is only about 100 miles long. Its greatest width is about 35 miles. Only one state is smaller. But Delaware's location has helped its people make it an important farming and manufacturing state.

Great highways and railroads link the northern end of Delaware directly with Washington, Baltimore, Philadelphia, and New York City. Boats, too, can carry cargoes between those big cities and Wilmington, Delaware's largest city. Fish caught along Delaware's coast and products of the little state's chicken farms, dairy farms, truck gardens, and fruit orchards help to feed the many millions of city people in nearby states.

The first colonists to make a lasting settlement in Delaware were a band of Swedes. In 1638, they founded Fort Christina where Wilmington now stands. They called the country round about "New Sweden." Many other Europeans came later. Among them were Finnish, Dutch, English, and Welsh people. Early settlers quickly saw the advantages of northern Delaware for manufacturing. In the 1700's their little

mills were busy at water-power sites. And the settlers were building ships along the Delaware River. Ships still are built there. In the early 1800's a Delawarean invented a flour milling machine and an engine to run it. Soon the mills of Wilmington were grinding wheat for Delaware, Pennsylvania, and Maryland farmers.

Today Delaware is world famous for its manufacture of chemical products. The well-known Du Pont company alone has three chemical plants in Delaware. The first Du Pont plant was a powder mill built near Wilmington in 1802. Wilmington is still a leader in the making of chemical goods. Among Delaware's chemical products are dyes, dental supplies, nylon, artificial rubber, paints, and varnishes. Paper and pulp, textiles, hardware, fine leather, cloth, and heavy machinery are made, too.

Along the Atlantic coast of southern Delaware is a vacation land of beaches, sand dunes, and summer cottages. But they are not as famous as the factories, farms, and some of the interesting, very early buildings still to be seen in the little first state in the Union.

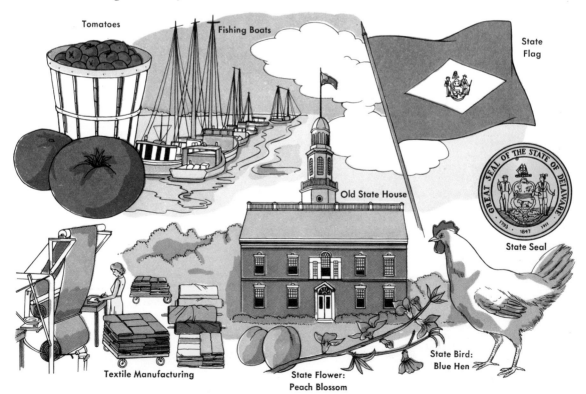

Tomatoes
Fishing Boats
State Flag
Old State House
State Seal
Textile Manufacturing
State Flower: Peach Blossom
State Bird: Blue Hen

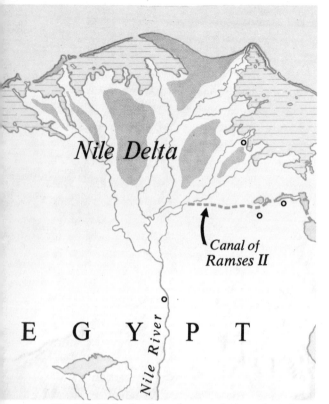

Nile Delta

↑ *Canal of Ramses II*

E G Y P T

Nile River

The Nile Delta has been famous since ancient times.

DELTA A river almost always carries a load of sand and mud and pebbles. Many rivers carry their loads to the sea. When the water of a river strikes the sea, it is slowed up. In most cases it cannot carry its load far. It drops first the pebbles, then the sand, and then the mud. It may drop so much that a fan of land is built up at the mouth of the river.

Such a fan of land is called a delta. It got its name because it is a little like the shape of the Greek letter called *delta*. Delta is the Greek letter from which our D came. It is shaped like this: △ .

In the Old World one of the most famous deltas is the delta of the Nile. Much of the fertile land of Egypt is in this delta. The delta helped ancient Egypt become one of the cradles of civilization.

In the United States there is a great delta at the mouth of the Mississippi River. The city of New Orleans is many miles north of this delta. But at one time the land where New Orleans stands was, scientists believe,

a part of the Mississippi delta. Over many centuries, the river kept on bringing down millions of tons of mud and sand to it each year. The mouth of the river—and its delta —kept moving farther and farther south. As more years continue to go by, the delta of the Mississippi is almost sure to extend even farther out into the Gulf of Mexico than it does now.

The Amazon, the Ganges, the Indus, and the Rhine are other rivers that have built up big deltas. Some rivers flow too swiftly to build a delta. The Congo is one.

Notice from the map how the Nile branches as it flows across its delta. Most rivers fan out in much the same way. (See AMAZON RIVER; EGYPT; MISSISSIPPI RIVER; NEW ORLEANS; NILE RIVER; RHINE RIVER; RIVERS.)

DEMOCRACY The word "democracy" comes from two Greek words that mean "people" and "rule." Democracy is a kind of government which lets people rule themselves. They rule themselves by choosing their rulers and their lawmakers. Abraham Lincoln told clearly what democracy means in his famous Gettysburg Address. He called it "government of the people, by the people, and for the people."

The idea of democracy is not new. The ancient Greeks chose their rulers. For a time the Romans did, too. Down through the Middle Ages some of the German tribes kept the idea of democracy alive. But in most countries where we find democracy today the people won the right to rule themselves by a hard struggle.

The United States is a republic. Its people elect most officials of the government—the lawmakers as well as other government officers. Many countries where the people rule themselves are republics. But some democracies have kings or queens. Their kings or queens, however, have no real power. The people of England, for example, rule themselves as in a republic although they have a king or queen.

LINCOLN AT GETTYSBURG

Lincoln asked for equal opportunity for all men.

Some countries claim that they are democracies when they really are not. They have elections, but there are no choices to be made. There is only one list of candidates for the people to vote for.

The Declaration of Independence of the United States says that everyone has a right to "life, liberty, and the pursuit of happiness." Democracy is based on this idea. But this idea is very different from the one that some people have—the idea that in a free country, as a democracy is often called, everyone can do as he pleases. No one has a right to do anything to harm others.

Democracy has its problems. It is not easy to choose leaders wisely. Some people do not do their fair share in ruling themselves. They may not, for instance, vote in an election. The people that are elected may do unwise things to make themselves popular. Besides, the machinery of a democracy is cumbersome when there is a crisis of some kind. It is much easier for one person to make a decision than for millions of people to make one through the people they elect. Many republics during the past half-century have fallen into the hands of dictators during a crisis.

In some countries that have become republics things have not gone well because the people were not used to making decisions for themselves. They were not used to the idea of democracy.

In the United States a person must reach a certain age (21 years in most states) to be able to vote and thus to take part in the government. But boys and girls can practice the ideas of democracy in their everyday lives. In clubs and classes they can elect their officers. They can learn to choose leaders wisely instead of just voting for their personal friends. They can practice listening to suggestions and considering them carefully, no matter who makes them. On the playground they can see that everyone has a fair chance, no matter what his race or religion may be, or how wealthy or poor his family may be. Boys and girls who practice democracy day by day will be better members of a democracy when they grow up to vote. (See CITIZENSHIP; COMMUNISM; DICTATORS; FASCISM; GOVERNMENT; NAZIS; SOCIALISM.)

The Bill of Rights signed in 1689 helped the cause of democracy.

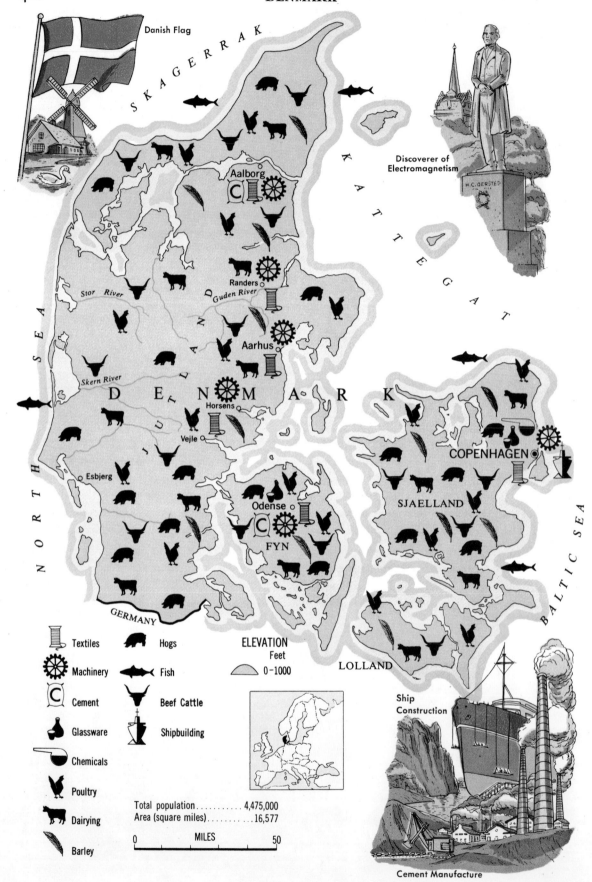

Danish Flag

Discoverer of
Electromagnetism

H.C.OERSTED

SKAGERRAK

KATTEGAT

NORTH SEA

Aalborg

Stor River

Randers

Guden River

Skern River

DENMARK

JUTLAND

Aarhus

Horsens

Vejle

Esbjerg

ODENSE

FYN

SJAELLAND

COPENHAGEN

BALTIC SEA

GERMANY

LOLLAND

ELEVATION
Feet
0–1000

Textiles

Machinery

Cement

Glassware

Chemicals

Poultry

Dairying

Barley

Hogs

Fish

Beef Cattle

Shipbuilding

Ship
Construction

Total population.......... 4,475,000
Area (square miles).......... 16,577

0   MILES   50

Cement Manufacture

DENMARK The name of this small country in northwestern Europe means "land of the Danes." Denmark is only half as large as Maine. But it has almost five times as many people. Part of Denmark is on a narrow peninsula stretching northward from Germany toward Norway and Sweden. About 500 islands nearby make up the rest of the country. No place in Denmark is more than 40 miles from the sea.

Danes were among the Vikings who made daring sea voyages very long ago. One far-off island they reached is now a Danish island named Greenland. It is larger than Denmark itself. But almost all of Greenland is covered with a great sheet of ice. Some Eskimos and a few Danes live in the fringe of land not covered by ice.

Denmark has little coal, no stores of metals to be mined, and sandy, rather poor soil. But it is not a poor country. It has enough rain, and mild summers and winters. Its people are well educated. They know how to build poor soil into much better soil. Making good use of what they have has made them prosperous.

A great many Danes own small farms and make a good living by raising cows, pigs, and chickens. England and other countries near by want to buy all the butter, meat, and eggs the Danish farmers have to sell. Those farmers take pride in being sure the things they sell are of the very best quality. They have found ways of improving their cows, pigs, and chickens. And farmers band together to sell their products and to buy what they have to buy. They get better prices for what they sell and pay less for what they buy than if each one did his own selling and buying.

Of course, not all the people of Denmark are farmers. Some of them work in the factories in Denmark's cities. They make chiefly things the Danish people themselves need. Like the Vikings of early times, other Danes spend much time on the sea. Each year Danish fishermen catch thousands of tons of fish. And there are many Danish merchant ships. The name of Denmark's one very large and famous city is Copenhagen, which in Danish means "merchant's haven." Almost a fourth of all the people of Denmark live in it.

Copenhagen is the capital of Denmark. The country is a kingdom. One of the sights of this great port is the palace of the king. Another of its many sights is the huge number of bicycles on the streets in rush hours. Hundreds of factory workers ride to and from their work on bicycles. Among its factories are those where the famous Copenhagen pottery is made.

The big city is on one of the islands that make up Denmark. Many big ships stop at its wharves on their way between the North Sea and the Baltic. It has shipbuilding yards. It is one of the great ports of Europe and of the world. (See BALTIC SEA; GREENLAND; NORTH SEA; VIKINGS.)

Royal Danish Ballet   Farming   Dairying   Fishing   Pottery

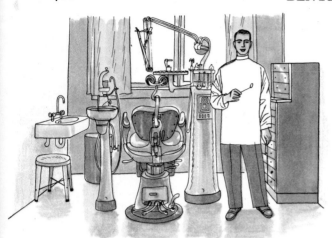

A dentist needs special equipment to do his work.

DENTISTRY Our teeth are an important part of our bodies. Without teeth we could eat only very soft food. And there are many words we could not pronounce clearly if we did not have teeth.

Sometimes our teeth give us trouble. A tooth may ache. Or an infection in our teeth or gums may make us feel sick all over. Doctors who treat teeth are called dentists. Their work is called dentistry.

Today dentists do marvelous things to help us save our teeth. They can treat aching teeth. They can straighten teeth that are crooked. They can put an artificial tooth in a place where a tooth has been lost. They can make whole sets of teeth for a person who has lost all his teeth. They can take X rays of teeth to find out whether there is any hidden trouble. If a tooth cannot be saved, they can pull it with little pain.

To dull pain when he has to pull a tooth a dentist often uses Novacain. It numbs the area around the tooth. He may also use Novacain to deaden the nerves when a deep cavity must be drilled.

Early people probably had much less trouble with their teeth than the people of today have. They ate coarse food that gave their teeth good exercise. But people have certainly needed dentists for many centuries. Dentistry, however, is rather new. There were no real dentists until about 250 years ago. And the first school for dentists was not founded until 1840.

In early times doctors treated teeth along with other parts of the body. But about all they knew to do for an aching tooth was to pull it or to put some kind of medicine on it. Some of these medicines were peculiar —tortoise blood, pills made of garlic and horseradish seeds and milk, and bones of the "sea dragon."

Magic was often called on to cure toothache. One magic charm was to say, when the moon was waning and when Mars and Jupiter could be seen, the words "argidam, margidam, sturgidam."

During the Middle Ages barbers took over the pulling of teeth. Some of them grew to be famous because they could pull teeth so skilfully.

To be a dentist today, a person must study for several years. In the United States he must go to college for at least two years and then he must attend a dental school for four years. He must take an examination in order to receive a license to practice, just as other doctors have to. After a dentist's name one often sees the letters "D.D.S." These letters stand for "Doctor of Dental Surgery."

Everyone owes it to himself to take care of his teeth. He should visit a dentist at least once a year. (See ANESTHETICS; FOODS; HEALTH; TEETH; X RAY.)

PARTS OF A TOOTH

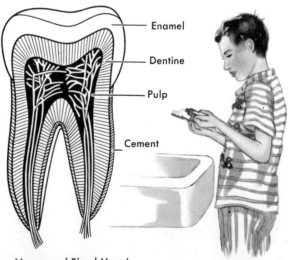

Enamel

Dentine

Pulp

Cement

Nerves and Blood Vessels

DEPARTMENT STORE GOODS

DEPARTMENT STORES A box of candy; a paper of pins; a book; a dress; a washing machine; an electric train; silk by the yard; a big armchair; a diamond ring; a set of fine china! All these things and hundreds of others, too, can be bought in a department store. Department stores get their name because they are made up of many shops, or departments. A department store is almost sure to have a toy department, a jewelry department, a dress-goods department, and so on.

The idea of department stores is not much more than 100 years old. Marshall Field and Company, one of the world's oldest and most famous department stores, celebrated its 100th anniversary in 1954. At the same time that Marshall Field was building his store in Chicago, John Wanamaker was building a department store in Philadelphia. The Marshall Field and Wanamaker stores paved the way for many others in cities across the land.

Before the days of department stores general stores handled groceries and hardware and goods by the yard. But they had only a little of everything. They were not at all like big department stores.

Most department stores have show windows. Even people who do not want to buy enjoy window shopping. At holiday time the stores are beautifully decorated.

Department stores make shopping easy. There are elevators or escalators to carry customers from floor to floor. There are rest rooms and tearooms. Besides, department stores make paying simple. They let customers charge what they buy and pay for it all at one time or so much each month.

Department stores work hard to please customers. They deliver goods free of charge, and make exchanges. They follow the idea that "the customer is always right." It was a rather new idea when department stores began. (See ELEVATOR.)

Section of a Department Store

This desert in New Mexico gleams with white sand.

DESERTS In the northern part of Chile several years may go by without a single drop of rain. There are not many parts of the world as dry as that. But large areas get very little rain or snow. We call such regions deserts.

In all deserts there is very little water for plants to use. But not all deserts are dry. In the Far North there are deserts even where there is much water in the soil. But a few inches below the top of the ground the water is always frozen. There are other deserts that have water, but it is too salty for plants to use. One such desert is near Great Salt Lake in Utah. But most people think of hot, dry deserts when they hear the word "desert." The Sahara in Africa is the world's largest hot, dry desert. The Gobi Desert in Asia is another very large one.

Such deserts usually have great stretches of bare sand. Winds pile up the sand into hills, or dunes. Scattered through the deserts there may be oases, where trees and other plants grow. Springs or streams fed by rain or snow far away furnish the needed water for green oases.

Night can be cold in a hot, dry desert. In the air there is very little water to act as a blanket, and the heat of the day escapes very fast as soon as the sun goes down. Scorching heat in the daytime and shivering cold at night is the rule.

Dry deserts, oddly enough, can have bad floods. Any rain that falls is likely to come in heavy showers, the kind we call cloudbursts. The rain cannot sink into the ground as fast as it falls. It rushes off into small streams and makes the streams overflow. Many travelers in a desert have been stopped by floods.

Often there are sandstorms in dry deserts. There is nothing to break the wind as it blows over the great stretches of sand.

Some plants and animals are fitted for living in deserts. The picture shows a few.

Some desert plants have very long roots that can get water from deep in the ground.

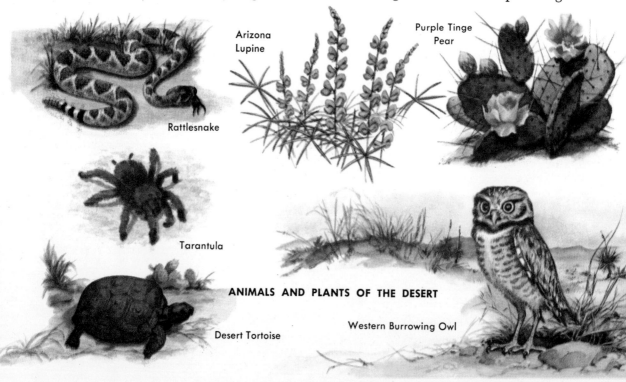

Rattlesnake

Arizona Lupine

Purple Tinge Pear

Tarantula

ANIMALS AND PLANTS OF THE DESERT

Desert Tortoise

Western Burrowing Owl

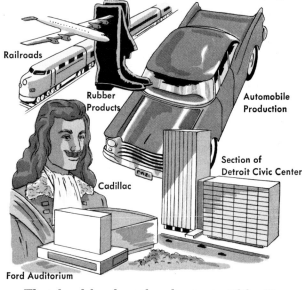

Ford Auditorium

Some have special ways of storing the water they get. They may have very thick leaves or stems. They may have a waxy covering that keeps the water in them from evaporating. Some are fitted for living in the desert because they can grow and bloom in a short time. After a rain the seeds of these plants sprout. They grow very fast, bloom, and form seeds. Seeds can live through months of dryness.

Desert animals, as a rule, need less water than other animals. Some of them never drink any water at all. Many animals of the desert hide during the day when the sun is hot. They come out at sundown to hunt for their food.

Many deserts are rich storehouses of minerals. Nitrate and borax are two of the minerals we get from desert lands. Some desert land can be turned into excellent farmland by irrigation. (See ADAPTATION TO ENVIRONMENT; CACTI; CAMELS AND CARAVANS; DEATH VALLEY; PAINTED DESERT; SAHARA.)

DETROIT Today Detroit, Mich., is the greatest automobile manufacturing city in the world. And it is the oldest of the Great Lakes cities. It was a French settlement from 1701 till 1760. Then it was a British settlement until the land on which it stands became part of the United States in 1796.

That land borders the short, straitlike Detroit River, on which boats must sail in going between Lakes Huron and Erie. *Détroit* is the French word for strait.

Many early settlers moving west by way of Lake Erie landed at Detroit. Some of them stayed there. Others moved on along roads leading westward from it. The settlement grew steadily. After 1818, when lake steamers first appeared on Lake Erie, Detroit grew faster than before. And since automobile manufacturing began there, in 1899, Detroit has grown very fast. It has become one of the very few American cities having more than 1,500,000 people.

In the early days of car making, there were several lake cities where steel, upholstery, rubber, glass, and other materials could be brought together at fairly low cost. But Detroit had workers already skilled in building carriages and motorboats. And one Detroit citizen, Henry Ford, decided to try making automobiles there. He had great success, and many automobile factories were built in the city. People going between the United States and Canada see some of Detroit's factories, boulevards, and fine buildings. Detroit is the largest city on the boundary between those countries. International Bridge crosses the Detroit River there. (See AUTOMOBILES; FORD, HENRY; GREAT LAKES; MICHIGAN.)

Dewdrops sparkle like jewels on a spider web.

DEW On sunshiny summer mornings the grass is often wet with dew. It may be so wet that it is hard to believe that there has not been a shower. There may be drops of dew on flowers and bushes and spider-webs, too. The drops of dew sparkle like jewels when the sun shines on them.

Drops of dew look like drops of rain. But they do not fall from clouds as rain-drops do. They are formed where they are found. They are formed from the water vapor in the air when moist air strikes something cold. Cold air cannot hold as much moisture as warm air.

Drops of water form on the outside of glasses of cold water or lemonade on hot summer days. They form when the warm, moist air strikes the cold glass. They are like drops of dew.

Dew is formed much oftener in fair weather than in cloudy weather. On clear nights things near the ground cool off much faster than on cloudy nights. Clouds act as a kind of blanket. Unless flowers and leaves and spiderwebs are cooler than the air, dew will not form on them.

Wind also keeps dew from forming. On a windy night the air is constantly moving about. None of it stays near the cool ground long enough to be cooled off and to lose some of its moisture.

Dew does not stay on very long after the sun comes up. The grass and other things on which the dew has formed soon get warm. Then the dew changes again to water vapor. This same water vapor may become dew again the next night if the weather is calm and fair. (See FROST.)

DIAMONDS Strange as it seems, black soot and brilliant diamonds are both carbon. Diamonds are crystals of carbon. Carbon crystals do not form unless the carbon is pressed very hard and heated very hot at the same time. The crystals are usually found deep in the ground. Perhaps the places where they are found are the throats of dead volcanoes. If so, the tops of these old volcanoes have been worn away by wind and water.

For many centuries most big diamonds came from India. Now the greatest diamond mines are in Africa.

The children of a poor Dutch farmer helped to discover that there are diamonds in Africa. One day in 1866, the children found a pretty pebble in a river near their home in Hopetown, South Africa. It looked like frosted glass, but in spots it glistened more than glass ever glistens. The children took it home with them. One day a neighbor saw it and offered to buy it. The children gave it to him for nothing. It turned out to be a big diamond.

When the word spread around, people began hunting for diamonds nearby, and they found them. Diamonds were later found in other parts of Africa.

GEM CUTS OF DIAMONDS

Marquise
Square
Brilliant
Pear Shape
Heart Shape
Square Cut (Jonker)
Baguettes

Discovery of the Jonker Diamond—1934

The diamonds of Africa are found in a rock that is called "blue ground." The rock is dug out, crushed, and mixed with mud. The diamonds are too hard to be hurt by the crushing machines. The mud and crushed rock are washed away, and the diamonds are left.

Mining diamonds is not pleasant work. The mines are so deep that it is very hot in them. Besides, the miners are not allowed to go home after a day's work. They have to live at the mines. Diamonds are worth so much for their size that a dishonest workman could carry home a fortune with him every day.

Diamonds are harder than anything else we know about. Their name comes from a Greek word that means "unconquerable." Little diamonds are set in tools for cutting or drilling through hard rock and metal. Big diamonds are used as jewels.

Before they are used as jewels, diamonds are cut and polished. The cutting and polishing have a great deal to do with how much a diamond sparkles.

The weight of a diamond is measured in carats. A one-carat stone is rather large for a ring. But it would take about 2,400 one-carat stones to weigh a pound.

The largest diamond ever found was named the Cullinan diamond. It was mined in South Africa in 1905. That country gave it as a present to Edward VII, king of England. It weighed 3,106 carats. It was cut into nine big diamonds and many small ones. The biggest of the gem stones was set in the king's scepter. The next largest one was set in his crown.

The Jonker diamond, found in 1934, was famous for its purity. It weighed 726 carats. This diamond was later cut into 12 flawless stones. Among the other famous diamonds are the Koh-i-noor, the Great Mogul, the Orloff, and the Star of the South.

Artificial diamonds can now be made in electric furnaces. But, so far, all the artificial diamonds that are being made are small. (See CARBON; GEMS; JEWELRY.)

DIATOMS The tiny one-celled green plants called diatoms are too small to be seen without a microscope. Diatoms are found in many places—in salt water, in fresh water, and in damp soil.

These tiny plants live in transparent shells made of silica, the material that is used in making glass. Each shell consists of two parts. These two parts fit together like the two parts of a pillbox.

When a diatom grows too big for its shell, it pushes the two halves of the shell apart. Then the little plant divides into two plants. One of the new plants stays in the top half of the shell. The other stays in the bottom half of the shell. Then each plant makes for itself the half of the shell that is missing.

Many fish eat diatoms. These tiny plants are rich food, for they have oil in them.

Diatoms have lived on the earth for a very, very long time. Scientists think that much of the oil we now get from the earth came from diatoms that lived millions of years ago. One kind of rock is made of diatom shells that fell to the bottom of ancient seas. This rock is sometimes ground up and used in making concrete.

Besides being useful, diatoms are beautiful. Some are round, some are oval, and some are three-sided. Others are like tiny new moons. Still others are star-shaped. All of them have beautiful markings on their shells. Under a good microscope they make a pretty picture. (See ALGAE; PLANKTON; PLANT KINGDOM.)

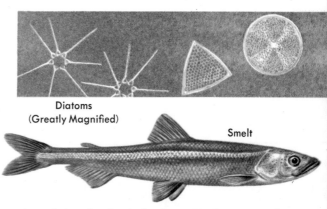

Diatoms
(Greatly Magnified)

Smelt

A smelt is only nine inches long, but in one mouthful it can swallow thousands of diatoms.

DICTATORS When one man becomes so powerful that he takes over the government of a country and decides how it shall be run, he is called a dictator. His rule is called a dictatorship. A dictatorship is just the opposite of a democracy.

A dictator usually has the country's army on his side. If he did not, it would be hard for him to take over the government. Sometimes a dictator may be popular with many of his people even though he does not let them rule themselves. But some dictators have been feared and hated by most of the people under them.

Many countries have had dictators. The list below names some recent ones and tells what countries they rule or ruled.

Name	Country	Ruled
Francisco Franco	Spain	1939-
Adolf Hitler	Germany	1933-1945
Mustapha Kemal	Turkey	1920-1938
Benito Mussolini	Italy	1922-1943
Juan D. Peron	Argentina	1946-1955
Antonio de Oliveira Salazar	Portugal	1932-
Joseph Stalin	U.S.S.R.	1928-1953
Marshall Tito (Josip Broz)	Yugoslavia	1945-

DIGESTION Our bodies are built of many millions of living cells. Every one of these cells needs food. The cells in our fingers need food just as much as the cells in the walls of our stomachs. The blood carries food to them all. Before the food we eat can get into the blood it must be changed to a liquid. The changing is called digestion.

Many parts of the body have a share in digesting our food. All together they are called the digestive system. The diagram at the right shows the digestive system.

It takes several different digestive juices to change all the kinds of food we eat into liquids. One of these juices is saliva. Saliva comes into our mouths from nearby glands and is mixed with the food as we chew.

When the food reaches the stomach, it is mixed with gastric juice, which comes from the stomach walls. Then in the small intestine three other juices help with digestion. They are bile, pancreatic juice, and intestinal juice. Bile comes from the liver. Pancreatic juice comes from the pancreas. Intestinal juice comes from the wall of the small intestine.

By the time the food has traveled through the small intestine, all of it has been digested that is going to be. It has soaked through the walls of the blood vessels in the wall of the intestine. The waste goes into the large intestine and then out of the body.

Other animals must digest their food, too. But most of them do not eat nearly as many kinds of food as we do. (See BLOOD; BODY, HUMAN; CELL; FOODS.)

DIGESTIVE SYSTEM

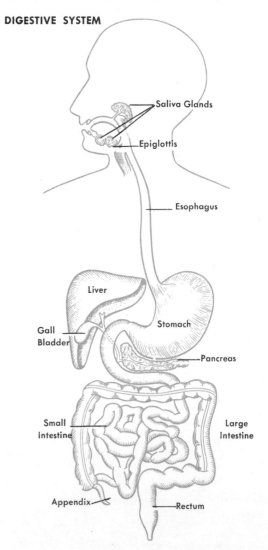

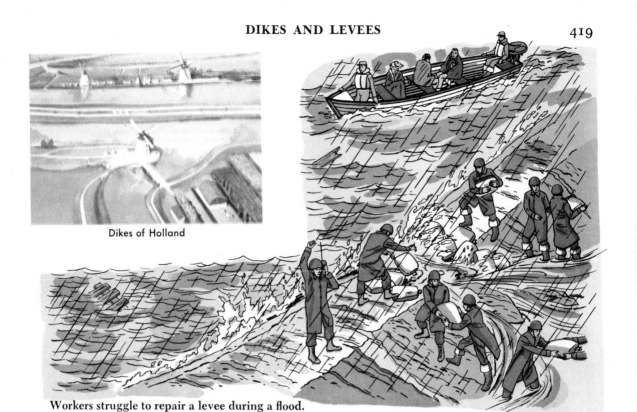

Dikes of Holland

Workers struggle to repair a levee during a flood.

DIKES AND LEVEES When there is low-land near a river or sea, the water some-times floods the land. In many places high banks have been built to shut the water out. These banks are often called dikes. "Levees" is another name for them.

Dikes are made mostly of clay. They may be partly concrete. Bundles of willow twigs are sometimes used to help hold the clay in place. Then grass is usually planted on the dikes. Trees or bushes may be planted on them, too. The roots of grass, bushes, and trees help keep the clay from being washed away.

Probably the most famous dikes in the world are those in the Netherlands. A great deal of the Netherlands is below sea level. The dikes keep the land from being flooded. Pumps work day and night to lift water out of the low, wet fields. There is a story of a Dutch boy who saw a little hole in one of the dikes. He knew it would get bigger and the dike would break. So he put his finger in the hole to hold the water back and waited for hours until help came.

Probably this story is not true. But a break in a dike may mean flooding much good land. Storks are carefully protected in the Netherlands, partly because they eat small furry animals that might burrow into the dikes. The people of the Netherlands purposely broke some of their dikes in World War II to stop the armies of their enemies. Some of their dikes were broken also in a great storm early in 1953.

Wherever dikes are built, they have to be watched. In flood time sandbags are rushed to places where there is danger that the dike will give way. Mats made of tree branches are used, too.

Along some rivers the dikes have to be made higher and higher as years go by. A river flowing between dikes may be carry-ing a great deal of mud. If the river slows down, it may have to drop some of its load in the river bed. The river bed grows high-er and higher. Then the dikes have to be made higher. At last the bed of the river may be higher than the land. The water is held in the river only by the dikes. It is easy to see what would happen if one of these dikes should break! (See FLOODS; HWANG HO; MISSISSIPPI RIVER; NETHERLANDS; RIVERS; WINDMILL.)

Stegosaurus

Allosaurus

Brontosaurus

DINOSAURS No one has ever seen a dinosaur. The last dinosaurs disappeared about 60 million years ago, long before there were any people on the earth. These ancient reptiles lived in the long, long period called the Age of Reptiles.

The word "dinosaur" means "terrible lizard." But dinosaurs were not lizards. They were not even very close relatives of the lizards. And though many of the dinosaurs were terrible, not all of them were.

There were more than 5,000 kinds of dinosaurs. Some were small, some were medium-sized, and some were giants. The largest were larger than any other animals that ever lived on land. They were not as big as the great whales of today, but they were far bigger than our elephants.

Brontosaurus (bron toe SO rus) was one of the giant dinosaurs. Its name means "thunder lizard." *Brontosaurus* was so big that it is supposed to have made a noise like thunder when it walked about. It spent most of its time in swamps eating the plants that grew there. The water in the swamps

The *Diplodocus* was the longest of the dinosaurs.

Triceratops

Tyrannosaurus

Trachodon

helped this giant hold up its great bulk. Stretching out from the huge body were a very long neck and a very long tail. From the end of its nose to the tip of its tail it was about 70 feet long. *Diplodocus* (di PLOD o kus), another giant, was even longer but was not so heavy. Ten of these huge reptiles walking in single file would have made a parade as long as a city block.

Brontosaurus and *Diplodocus* were gentle beasts. So was the duck-billed dinosaur *Trachodon* (TRAK o don). They ate nothing but plants. But some of the dinosaurs were flesh eaters. They were the terrible reptiles. *Allosaurus* (al o SO rus) was a flesh eater. *Tyrannosaurus* (ti RAN o so rus) was another, and probably the most terrible of all. It was 18 to 20 feet tall and had teeth several inches long. It walked on its hind legs and used the sharp claws on its front feet to help kill other animals.

Some of the plant-eating dinosaurs had armor that helped to protect them from the flesh eaters. *Stegosaurus* (steg o SO rus)

had a double row of plates down its back and sharp spikes on its tail. *Triceratops* (tri SER a tops) had three horns and a frill of bone around its neck.

The dinosaurs were all stupid creatures. They did not have much room in their heads for brains. *Brontosaurus* weighed about 35 tons, but its brain weighed less than a pound.

We know about dinosaurs chiefly through their bones and their footprints in the rocks. Scientists have found, too, the petrified eggs of *Protoceratops* (pro to SER a tops), a small armored dinosaur.

No one knows exactly why the dinosaurs disappeared. Changes in climate probably had a great deal to do with their disappearance. The mammals first appeared in the Age of Reptiles and they may have eaten dinosaur eggs. But why the dinosaurs all disappeared when other reptiles—lizards, turtles, crocodiles, and the tuatara—lived on is a puzzle. (See FOSSILS; LIFE THROUGH THE AGES; REPTILES.)

DIOGENES The philosopher Diogenes lived in ancient Greece more than 2,000 years ago. Diogenes believed that everyone should lead a very simple life. He gave away most of his possessions. For a while he even lived in a big tub to show that people did not have to have all the comforts they were used to.

Many stories were told about Diogenes. Here are three of them:

One day Diogenes walked through the streets of Athens carrying a lighted lantern. People asked him what he was doing with the lantern. His answer was, "I am hunting for an honest man."

Diogenes gave away all his possessions except a cloak, a purse, and a cup. One day he watched a small boy make his hands into a cup and dip up water with them. Diogenes saw that he did not really need a cup and threw his away.

Diogenes once met Alexander the Great. Alexander said that he would grant any favor Diogenes asked of him. "All I ask," said Diogenes, "is that you do not stand between me and the sun." Alexander liked this answer. "If I were not Alexander," he said, "I should wish to be Diogenes."

Diogenes searched for an honest man.

A scene in a well-planned diorama is very lifelike.

DIORAMA The picture above shows a diorama. A diorama is much like a small stage. The background is painted just as it is on a stage. But there are no actors that move on and off. Instead there are models that stay in place. In a good diorama it is not easy to see where the models end and the background begins.

Dioramas are common in museums. For many exhibits they are more effective than pictures would be. (See MUSEUMS.)

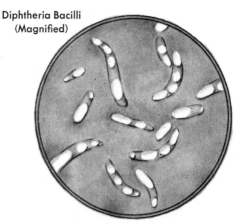

Diphtheria Bacilli (Magnified)

DIPHTHERIA (dif THEER e a) Every disease has certain signs, or symptoms. Among the symptoms of diphtheria are a very sore throat and a fast pulse.

For many years diphtheria was one of the most dreaded of all diseases. Now it is far less feared because doctors have ways of both fighting it and preventing it. Most cases of diphtheria can be cured by a drug called an antitoxin. Of course, it is better to prevent a disease than to cure it. Many children, before they are a year old, are given shots to protect them from diphtheria and certain other diseases. Before they go to school they are given booster shots to keep them safe.

Diphtheria is very contagious. The germs, or rod-shaped bacilli, that cause it may even go "hitchhiking" in the throat of a well person who has had the disease at some time in the past. Fortunately, only a few well people normally carry these germs around. The people who do are called carriers. As a rule they do not guess that they may give a disease to other people. (See BACTERIA; DISEASES.)

DISEASE GERMS In early times many people believed that diseases were caused by witches or demons. Sick people were sometimes put in prison to drive out the evil spirits. Night air and bad odors were often blamed, too. Not until about 100 years ago did anyone blame disease germs. It was not even known that there were such things. Now we are sure that many of our diseases are caused by germs. We know that many other animals and many plants have germ diseases, too.

Some disease germs are bacteria—tiny plants far too small to be seen without a microscope. They are not green like most plants. They have no color at all. Some of them are round; some are shaped like little rods; and some are twisted. Bacteria are so very small that one alone could not possibly do much harm. But they grow and form new bacteria very fast. It may take one only 20 minutes to grow and divide into two plants. At this rate several million germs could come from one in a day's time.

Some disease germs are tiny one-celled animals called protozoa. Most of these tiny animals cannot be seen without a microscope, but they are bigger than bacteria.

Some disease germs are viruses. They are so small that they can be seen only with a special microscope called an electron microscope. Viruses are a great puzzle. They seem to be on the borderline between living things and things that are not alive. They can cause many diseases.

The chart below names some of the diseases bacteria, protozoa, and viruses cause.

Diseases Caused by Bacteria	Diseases Caused by Protozoa	Diseases Caused by Viruses
Diphtheria	Malaria	Colds
Tuberculosis	Amebic dysentery	Measles
Pneumonia	Tropical fever	Mumps
Typhoid fever	Tick fever	Poliomyelitis
Lockjaw	Sleeping sickness	Influenza
Undulant fever	Texas fever	Virus pneumonia
Pinkeye	(cattle)	Chickenpox
Scarlet fever		German measles
Cholera (hogs)		Foot-and-mouth
Anthrax (sheep)		disease (cattle)
Bang's disease		Mosaic (plants)
(cattle)		
Fire blight		
(fruit trees)		

Disease germs cause sickness in **different** ways. Some give off poisons as they grow. Others actually destroy some of the cells in the body of the plant or animal.

When germs get into our bodies, we have a whole army ready to attack them—the army of white cells in our blood. Our bodies produce chemicals, too, that act against the poisons germs make. We usually win a fight with germs, but not always. A big part of medicine today is finding ways to help our bodies fight germs. (See BACTERIA; DISEASES; MICROSCOPE; PARASITES; PASTEUR, LOUIS; PROTOZOA.)

DISEASE GERMS

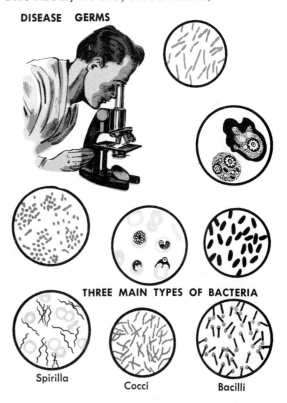

THREE MAIN TYPES OF BACTERIA

Spirilla   Cocci   Bacilli

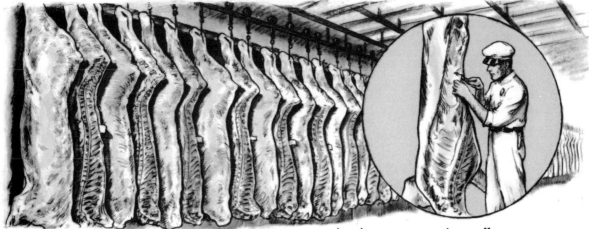

Sides of Beef in Cold Storage

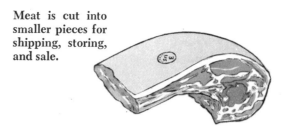

An inspector examines all meat for signs of disease. If it is healthy, it is graded and stamped with this seal.

Meat is cut into smaller pieces for shipping, storing, and sale.

DISEASES At this very moment millions of people in the world are sick, and they are sure to be sick with different diseases.

Some diseases we can get only from other people who have them. No one, for instance, can get mumps except from another person who has mumps. Mumps is one of the contagious diseases. To get a contagious disease, a person must be with someone who has the disease or he must handle something that a person with the disease has handled.

Other diseases come in a roundabout way from other people who have them. Sleeping sickness, for example, is carried from sick people to well people by a tiny insect, the tsetse (TSET see) fly. A number of other diseases are carried by insects. Malaria, bubonic plague, and typhus are three. Diseases can also be carried in impure water and impure milk.

Almost all the diseases that go from person to person are caused by disease germs. The germs may be very, very tiny plants called bacteria. They may be very, very tiny animals called protozoa. They may be viruses, which are even smaller than bacteria and protozoa. Viruses are so small that they are difficult to study. Scientists are working hard to find out more about them. Germs are also the cause of some diseases that do not spread from sick

people to well people. Lockjaw is one of a number of such diseases.

Plants and animals too big to be called germs cause some diseases. Tiny worms can be blamed for several diseases. One of these diseases comes from worms sometimes found in raw pork. Poison ivy and the mold that causes ringworm are among the larger disease-producing plants.

Several diseases are caused not by something we have but by something we haven't. Our foods must furnish us with a great many kinds of materials. We may get sick because some material which we should get from our food is missing. The material that is missing is likely to be some mineral or some vitamin. A child may have rickets because he is not getting enough calcium. A grownup may have scurvy because he is not getting enough vitamin C.

We may have a disease because some of the glands in our bodies are not working as they should. Diabetes is a disease of this kind. Sometimes some of the cells of which our bodies are built go on a rampage and grow in an unusual way. They may cause the disease we know as cancer.

Some diseases come from the kind of work people do. Coal miners may get a serious disease of the lungs from breathing too much coal dust. Men who work day after day with lead without the proper protection may get lead poisoning.

Our minds as well as other parts of our bodies may be sick. Mental diseases come about in different ways. We do not know nearly as much as we would like to know about what causes them.

We have worked out good ways of fighting diseases. Even the contagious diseases that almost all children used to have are not as common as they once were. Many contagious diseases are prevented by vaccination or by "shots." Contagious diseases are all kept down by keeping sick people away from well ones. We have learned to fight diseases so well that today we can expect to live three or four times as long as our cave-man ancestors.

Eating well-balanced meals and keeping clean help us to remain healthy and free from disease.

Of course, people are not the only living things that have diseases. All plants and animals have them. Even bacteria can be killed by a virus. Cats and dogs have distemper. Hog cholera is a common disease of hogs. Tuberculosis is found among dairy cows. Psittacosis is parrot fever. Potato scab and fire blight are two of the many plant diseases. We have learned to fight the diseases that do harm to the plants and animals we raise just as we have learned to fight our own. (See BACTERIA; CANCER; DISEASE GERMS; FOODS; HEALTH; INSECT PESTS; PARASITES; PROTOZOA; VITAMINS.)

Milk, as well as many of our other foods, is tested in laboratories for purity before it is sent to market.

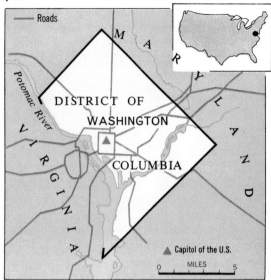

Roads

M A R Y L A N D

DISTRICT OF
WASHINGTON

COLUMBIA

Potomac River

V I R G I N I A

▲ Capitol of the U.S.

MILES
0   5

DISTRICT OF COLUMBIA The tiny part of eastern United States called the District of Columbia was named in honor of Christopher Columbus. It is on the Potomac River, and is between Maryland and Virginia. The District is not a part of any state. It belongs to the whole country. Its boundaries are also the boundaries of Washington, the nation's capital. Its area is about 69 square miles. About 900,000 people live in the District.

This is the story of the District of Columbia: Before George Washington was made the first president of the United States, a plan for governing the new country had been worked out. It is called the Constitution. It says that the government of the country must be carried on in a district, not more than 100 square miles in size, which is under the direct control of the Congress of the United States. The state of Maryland ceded to the United States the land now in the District.

At first, the new country along the Atlantic stretched from northernmost New Hampshire to southernmost Georgia. The location selected is halfway between. George Washington took part in choosing it. But John Adams was president by the time new buildings needed for government work were ready to be used. (See UNITED STATES; WASHINGTON, D.C.)

DIVING Probably diving is almost as old as swimming. At least we know that for centuries men have been diving down into the sea to find pearls and sponges. With the help of a heavy ball to weight him down a pearl diver may go 50 or 60 feet below the surface. Sponge divers with their collecting baskets sometimes go down as far.

In famous stories we read about dives down below the surface of the sea. We read, for instance, in a story more than 1,000 years old how Beowulf dove to the bottom of the sea to battle with the mother of the monster Grendel.

Today visitors who cruise along the shores of warm seas often throw pennies into the water to watch native boys dive for them. The boys do the kind of diving that has been done along the world's seacoasts for a very long time.

Fancy diving is rather new. It has become popular only within the past 75 years. Now fancy diving events are a part of the Olympic games and of many other athletic contests. In fancy diving the diver usually plunges into the water headfirst. But there are fancy dives in which the diver goes feet first into the water.

For a plain front dive, the diver holds his arms above his head with his hands together. His palms should not touch each other. His thumbs should touch, but both of his palms should face forward. His hands will strike the water first, and his arms will help protect his head. In a good dive there is very little or no splash as the diver hits the water.

To get himself into the air a diver usually uses a springboard. For a plain front dive he should spring up into the air about two-thirds as high as he is tall. Springing upward gives him a better chance to get into a good position for hitting the water.

The pictures show some of the many other kinds of dives. Diving takes a great deal of skill and practice.

A clumsy diver may hurt himself by striking the water flat instead of cutting his

Swan Dive

Open Pike

Closed Pike

Line-up
Foot First Entry

Back Dive

One-and-one-half
Cutaway

Line-up
Head First
Entry

FORMS OF FANCY DIVING

DODO The dodo is one of the birds that no one will ever see alive. It disappeared nearly 300 years ago.

This big bird lived on two islands in the Indian Ocean. For a time the sailors who stopped at these islands saw the dodo in great numbers. They found that they could kill it easily. The bird could not fly away when someone came near, for its wings were not strong enough to lift it off the ground. But it did not even run away. It did not know enough to try to save itself.

The sailors killed many dodoes to eat. Pigs and monkeys killed others. Before long there were none left. The dodo is now remembered chiefly for its stupidity. (See BIRDS OF YESTERDAY.)

way into it with his hands and head. A careless diver may hurt himself seriously. Many swimmers are badly injured every year by diving into water that is too shallow.

Skin diving is a new type of diving. Skin divers use special equipment so that they can stay below the surface long enough to have fun exploring.

When some people hear the word "diving" they think of deep-sea diving. Deep-sea diving is not at all like fancy diving and much of it is very different from skin diving. (See DEEP-SEA EXPLORING; PEARLS; SKIN DIVING.)

The heavy dodo could not fly.

Dogs descended from this catlike animal, *Cynodictis*.

DOGS The dog was the first wild animal to be tamed. Cave men had tame dogs many thousands of years ago.

Dogs and wolves are very close relatives. In fact, scientists believe that the wild ancestors of dogs were wolves.

Probably the taming of dogs began when some cave man brought home a wolf cub he had found. The cub grew up in the cave and was friendly. It was helpful, too. The wolf dog could drive away cave bears and other wild animals. This story, of course, is only a guess.

In dog shows today dogs of more than a hundred kinds, or breeds, are shown. A cave man would certainly be surprised if he could see them. Some still show their relationship to the wolf. Siberian huskies and German shepherds, for instance, do. But many of our dogs of today do not look at all like wolves. If a cave man could see a poodle or a Skye terrier or a Chihuahua (che WA wa), he might not even guess that it was a dog.

But there is a reason back of every kind of dog we have. Over the centuries people found many ways in which dogs could be helpful. They could help hunt. They could pull loads. Dogs could help herd cattle and sheep. They could guard their masters and their masters' property. Most important of all, they are good companions. It is easy to see that some breeds are better for helping in one way and other breeds for helping in another way. A Chihuahua, for instance, would not be very helpful at pulling loads.

So we now have big dogs and little dogs, smooth-haired dogs and shaggy ones, fast dogs and slow ones, playful dogs and dignified ones. Even the bark has been bred out of certain dogs. The reasons for developing some kinds of dogs are rather odd. The Greeks developed tiny lapdogs. They were meant to be held in a lady's lap to help keep her stomach warm. Bulldogs with huge jaws and short noses were developed so that they could hang on to the throat of a bull and still be able to breathe.

At shows dogs are divided into six groups: sporting, non-sporting, working, hound, terrier, and toy. Many breeds belong to each group. The pictures show dogs of some of the different breeds.

There are fashions in dogs just as there are fashions in clothes. Every kind of dog has many good points. But for one reason or another, a breed that has been popular for years may become less popular and some other breed may take its place. In the United States these dogs have been the most popular at one time or another since 1900: St. Bernard, English setter, collie, Boston terrier, Airedale, German shepherd, and cocker spaniel. Recently the boxer, the beagle, and the Chihuahua have become very popular. The dachshund, the poodle, and the Pekingese are now well liked, too.

Not many years ago people found a new way in which dogs can be helpful. "Seeing eye" dogs are trained to guide blind people. These dogs give us one more reason for calling the dog "man's best friend." (See ANIMAL BREEDING; DOMESTICATED ANIMALS; PETS.)

THE DOG FAMILY

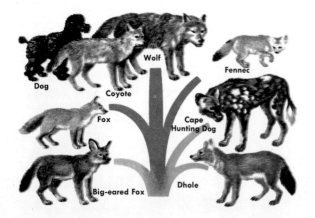

BREEDS OF DOGS

Great Pyrenees

Pointer

Samoyed

Irish Wolfhound

English Setter

Dalmatian

Bull Terrier

Siberian Husky

West Highland
White Terrier

Greyhound

Welsh Corgi

Sealyham Terrier

Skye Terrier

Old English Sheepdog

Weimaraner

Poodle

Doberman
Pinscher

Golden Retriever

Bloodhound

English Springer
Spaniel

Irish Terrier

Schnauzer

Whippet

Welsh Terrier

Gordon Setter

English Bulldog

Chihuahua

Boston Terrier

Keeshond

Saint Bernard

Great Dane

DOLLS For thousands of years children have played with dolls. Dolls have been found in the tombs of ancient Egypt. They have been found in the ruins of the cities of ancient Babylonia. Dolls have even been found in the graves of people who lived before anyone could write.

Many of the dolls American children play with look like real babies. They are as soft and cuddly as real babies, too. They can cry and say, "Mama." There are older dolls, too. Some can walk. Some have real hair that can be shampooed and curled. But probably no American girl loves her doll any more than a little girl of ancient Egypt loved her painted wooden doll with hair made of clay beads.

Even today the dolls children play with in some parts of the world look strange to children in other parts of the world. And homemade dolls are often very different from the dolls for sale in toy shops.

Materials of many kinds are used for dolls. Among them are plastics, rubber, china, wood, rags, and even cornhusks.

Some of the dolls in the toy stores of America were made in other lands. But many of them were made in the United States. The United States now makes more dolls than any other country in the world.

The stores that sell dolls usually sell doll houses and doll furniture, too. It is easy to spend hundreds of dollars for a doll house and its furniture. Probably the most famous doll house in the world is Colleen Moore's. Colleen Moore is a former movie actress. Her doll house is now in a museum in Chicago. (See TOYS.)

DOMESTICATED ANIMALS All the animals in the picture are domesticated animals. Domesticated animals are animals that have been tamed.

No one knows who first discovered that some wild animals could be tamed and raised. We do know that the discovery came about back in the days when most tools and weapons were still being made of stone. At about the same time that animals were first tamed, plants were tamed, too. The taming of animals and plants was important for several reasons. One big reason was that people no longer had to spend most of their time hunting for food.

Thinking of a big city like New York helps us see how important it was to find out that animals and plants could be raised for food. Imagine all the millions of people in New York starting out in the morning to shoot deer or rabbits and to gather roots and berries!

But not all our domesticated animals were tamed to furnish food. We do not eat dogs and cats. They do not furnish milk for us to use. Probably they were first tamed to be companions. Later, dogs helped with the hunt and learned to guard property. In time some were trained to pull sleds or carts, and much later to act as eyes for blind people. Cats came to be liked for their help in killing rats and mice.

Camels, donkeys, and llamas were tamed to be beasts of burden. Perhaps horses were, too. But they may have been raised first for food.

Although sheep were first raised for their meat, people soon found that their wool makes good cloth. People also found that the skins of cattle and goats and pigs make good leather.

Of course, people tamed animals that lived round about them. It is no wonder, then, that different animals were tamed in different parts of the world. The llama and the alpaca of South America help man in the same ways as do the reindeer in the Far North and the yak in Tibet.

Some domesticated animals are still found only in the parts of the world where they were once wild. Others have been carried far and wide. Of the animals we raise in the United States all except the turkey were brought from the Old World.

People should not be too proud of themselves because they have domesticated animals. For ants and termites have them, too. The domesticated animals of the ants and termites are other insects. Ants, for instance, have "ant cows" that they take good care of. These ant cows are small insects called aphids. The aphids give off little drops of a liquid called "honeydew." The ants eat it. In all, ants and termites have about 1,000 kinds of domesticated animals. (See CAMELS AND CARAVANS; CATS; CATTLE; DOGS; GOATS; HOOFED ANIMALS; HORSES; PIGS; POULTRY; SHEEP; YAK; ZEBU.)

DOMESTICATED ANIMALS OF MANY LANDS

Elephant

Camel

Water Buffalo

Llama

Yak

Sheep

Pony

Hunting Dog

Reindeer

Work Dog

Pig

Cow

Mule

Goat

Burro

Fishing Cormorant

Cat

Rabbit

Chicken

Guinea Hen Duck

Stephen A. Douglas

DOUGLAS, STEPHEN A. (1813-1861)
Every time a new president of the United
States is elected, at least one other person
is defeated. When Abraham Lincoln was
elected president, Stephen A. Douglas was
the candidate who was defeated.

Douglas had a nickname. It was "The
Little Giant." He got his nickname because
he was very short but had a big head and
big shoulders. He had an excellent voice
and made many wonderful speeches.

In 1858, two years before Lincoln defeated Douglas, Douglas had defeated Lincoln. But then they were running for sen-
ator, not president. Lincoln and Douglas
traveled all over Illinois to tell the voters
what their ideas were. They had many debates. These debates were of great interest
to the whole country. Douglas persuaded
the voters of Illinois that his ideas
were better than Lincoln's. He won the
election to the U.S. Senate.

But the tables were turned in the race for
president. Because of the stand Douglas
took on the slavery question, he made the
Southern Democrats angry. When it came
time to choose a president, these Southern-
ers refused to vote for him. Lincoln won.

Soon after the election, the War between
the States began. Douglas offered to help
Lincoln in any way he could. But he had
little chance to do so. He died from typhoid
fever only two months after the beginning
of the war. (See LINCOLN, ABRAHAM.)

DRAKE, SIR FRANCIS (1540-1596)
Queen Elizabeth I, the famous Queen of
England, sent her sailors far and wide to
explore the seven seas. The one who went
farthest was Francis Drake. He went clear
around the world!

Drake, nicknamed "The Dragon," was
very bold. He captured many ships belong-
ing to other countries and took a great deal
of treasure. Drake came very close to being
a pirate. But he captured the treasure for
his Queen and country, not for himself.

Drake's own ship was the "Golden Hind."
It was, of course, a sailing vessel. On his
ship Drake's men treated him like a king.

Drake was really the first leader of an
exploring party to sail all the way around
the world. Earlier, the ships of the Portuguese captain Magellan went around the
world, but Magellan died on the voyage.

Even if he had not sailed around the
world, Drake would be famous, f or he was
in charge of the English ships that defeated
the Spanish Armada. This was a great fleet
the Spanish King had sent to make war on
England. The sailors of other lands knew
what a great fighter and sailor Drake was.
The captain of one of the ships in the Spanish Armada gave up his ship as soon as he
found out that Drake, the Dragon, was on
the ship he was fighting. Drake did more
than any other person to make England the
ruler of the seas. (See ARMADA; ELIZA-
BETH I; MAGELLAN.)

Sir Francis Drake Being Knighted by his Queen

DRUGS All cities, large towns, and even most small towns have drugstores. The drugs these stores sell are chemicals that help people get well or keep well. Medicines are made of drugs. A medicine may have only one drug in it or it may be a combination of several different drugs.

Some drugs come from plants. Penicillin, for instance, comes from a little mold plant called penicillium. Some drugs come from animals. Cortisone comes from certain animal glands. Other drugs come from the earth. Sulfur is one of them. Scientists are producing still other drugs from chemicals in their laboratories. Year after year new drugs are discovered.

Certain drugs are called narcotics. A person may take one of these drugs for so long that finally his body cannot get along without it. In the end, such a drug may do him a great deal of harm.

DRUMS Even our cave-man ancestors had drums. Their drums were hollow logs with skins stretched across the open ends. All down through the ages drums have been used. Soldiers have marched into battle to the sound of drums. Dancers have danced to the rhythm of drums. Drums have been important in religious rites. Today they are an important part of all bands and most orchestras.

The tambourine is a small, shallow drum. It has only one "head," as the skin stretched across a drum is called. Metal disks, or jingles, are fastened loosely to the sides of a tambourine. A snare drum has two heads. Across the lower head strings of catgut, called snares, are fastened.

These snares produce a sharp, rattling sound as the drummer beats the drum. The player uses two thin hardwood drumsticks.

A bass drum is like a snare drum except that it is much bigger. Some college bands have bass drums so big that they have to be mounted on wheels. The player uses only one drumstick, but he may choose any of three kinds. The end may be covered with soft lamb's wool, with felt, or with leather. One covered with lamb's wool gives the most muffled sound, and one covered with leather the sharpest.

Kettledrums, or timpani, are found in almost all big orchestras. They are so named because they are shaped like big metal kettles. They have only one head. A kettledrum cannot be carried about.

Early explorers in Africa were surprised to find that the tribes and chieftains they visited had almost always received word of their coming. They did not know that the Africans could send drum messages. "Drum talk" was used long before wireless.

In the dead of night the sound of a good drum can be heard in the African jungles for 10 or even 15 miles. It takes skill to send messages on a drum. The messages have to be sent in code. A good drummer becomes widely known. An old African proverb tells a drummer not to eat chicken wings. A chicken makes little noise with its wings. The proverb suggests that if a drummer eats chicken wings, his messages will not go far. (See BAND; ORCHESTRA.)

DRUMS

The egg-laying duckbill is a mammal.

DUCKBILL It is easy to see how this animal got its name. Its bill is much like a duck's bill. It has webbed feet, too, and it lays eggs. But the duckbill is not a relative of the ducks. It is not even a bird. It has four legs instead of two and fur instead of feathers. It belongs to the big group of animals called mammals.

The duckbill is found wild only in Australia and on the nearby island of Tasmania. For many years it was not even found in zoos in other countries. It is a shy animal not easy to care for in captivity.

Some of the early settlers in Australia sent a few duckbill skins to some scientists in England. The scientists thought these settlers were playing a joke on them and had fastened the bills of some bird to the skins of animals!

In Australia there were once many more duckbills than there are now. Many were killed for their beautiful fur. Now there are laws to protect them.

Duckbills spend most of their time in the water. They can swim and dive very well. They eat worms, crayfish, and other small animals. In the banks of the streams where they live they dig long tunnels for their nests. A mother duckbill usually lays only one or two eggs at a time.

Although a duckbill is nearly two feet long, counting its tail, its eggs are tiny— less than an inch long. The baby duckbills of course are very tiny when they hatch. But they grow fast. They get milk from their mother just as all other baby mammals do. When they are very small, the mother holds them in place with her tail while they are getting their dinner.

The duckbill has another name. It is platypus. Sometimes the animal is called the duckbill platypus. (See AUSTRALIA.)

DUNES A dune is a hill of sand. Dunes are found along shores of lakes and oceans and in sandy deserts. Some of the biggest dunes in the world are on the shores of Lake Michigan.

Dunes are built by the wind. A small plant may start a dune. Wind carrying a load of sand strikes the little plant and drops part of its load. The sand forms a tiny hill in front of the plant. Now the wind strikes the tiny hill and drops more sand. Little by little the hill grows.

In one way dunes are very different from other hills—they go traveling. The wind blows sand up one side of the hill and over the top. The sand rolls down on the other side. In this way the dune slowly moves. Sometimes a moving dune buries a forest. Sometimes it moves on past and leaves a forest graveyard behind it.

There are many dunes that are no longer traveling. This is the story of almost every dune that has stopped moving: A newer dune first shut off much of the wind. Then small plants began to grow on the old dune. These plants helped protect the surface sand from the wind. Bigger plants could then grow and hold the dune in place. Some dunes have forests on them.

Some sand dunes of New Mexico rise 600 feet.

DUST Housekeepers spend a great deal of time dusting. Dust settles from the air and may make a gray coating over everything in a house.

How surprised many housekeepers would be if they knew that part of the dust they wipe off the floors and furniture each day is alive! But it is. Dust is made up

In hot, dry areas whirlwinds may form dust storms.

partly of tiny bits of rock. It may have in it bits of dead wood and dried leaves. It may have in it ashes from volcanoes—ashes from volcanoes have been blown clear around the world. It may have in it, too, particles left when a shooting star burned up on its way to the ground. It is almost sure to have some soot in it. But it also has in it yeasts and bacteria, and perhaps spores from several kinds of plants, and pollen from flowers. These are alive!

Yeasts are very tiny plants. They are much too small to be seen without a microscope. Bacteria are tiny plants which are even smaller than yeasts. Some of them are disease germs. Mushrooms and molds and ferns are three of the kinds of plants that have spores. These plants do not have seeds. They are scattered by spores instead. Pollen is the powder in flowers that helps form seeds.

In a region where there has not been enough rain, there may be great dust storms. The dust blown about in these storms is mostly topsoil. (See BACTERIA; DISEASE GERMS; FERNS; MOLDS; MUSHROOMS; POLLINATION; YEASTS.)

DWARFS Common marigolds grow to be about two feet tall. But some marigolds are never more than a few inches tall even when they are full grown. They are called dwarf marigolds.

Most people grow to be more than five feet tall. But some are less than four feet tall even when they are grown men and women. They are dwarfs. There are dwarfs among many kinds of plants and animals.

No one knows the whole story of why dwarfs appear. We do know that certain body glands, when they do not work properly, cause some people to become dwarfs.

In the great days of kings and queens many court jesters were dwarfs. Dwarfs were thought to be especially clever.

The most famous dwarf in America was "General Tom Thumb." His real name was Charles Stratton. He was given the name of Tom Thumb when P. T. Barnum persuaded him to join his circus. General Tom Thumb was 40 inches tall; he weighed 70 pounds. A famous English dwarf, Jeffrey Hudson, was much smaller. He was only 18 inches tall. This dwarf was in the court of Charles I of England.

There are many storybook dwarfs. Rumpelstilskin is one. The Seven Dwarfs in the story of Snow White are others.

At times it is a big help to be a dwarf. During World War II, for instance, dwarfs could work inside airplane parts in places too cramped for normal-sized workmen. (See BARNUM, P. T.; GIANTS; JESTERS.)

Often kings had dwarfs as attendants.

SOURCES OF DYES

Murex Shell

Crocus

Phoenicians Dyeing Robes

Sunflower

Oak Gall

Cochineal

Mud and Sulfur

Grapes

Hickory Nuts

Wool

Cotton

Modern Method of Dyeing Cloth

DYES Three thousand years ago the Phoenicians were the world's great traders. They sailed their ships far and wide from their home at the eastern end of the Mediterranean Sea. One of the goods they had to trade was a dye called Tyrian purple. "Phoenicia" is Greek for "land of the purple." The dye came from a small sea snail. The color was so beautiful—it was really crimson instead of purple—that rulers wanted it for their robes.

Long before the time of the Phoenicians people had found they could make dyes from some of the plants and animals around them. A person did not have to be very clever to get the idea of coloring cloth with the juices of beautiful berries. But it took years of experimenting to get good dyes. Some quickly faded. Others changed color in sunlight.

Some of the best dyes must have been discovered by accident. Tyrian purple is a good example. The dye came from a thick, bad-smelling white liquid just back of a snail's head. It turned green when exposed to light. Then it turned blue. Not till it was treated with weak lye did it turn to a beautiful red color.

Through the centuries dyes were made from bark, flowers, berries, nuts, roots, insects, shellfish, lichens, and plant galls. Indigo (blue), logwood (black), and saffron (yellow) were a few of the dyes.

In 1856 an English schoolboy made a great discovery. The boy, William Perkins, was carrying on an experiment during his Easter vacation. He was trying to get quinine from coal. He did not succeed. But he did get a lavender dye from coal tar. Soon scientists found that dyes of all colors can be made from coal tar. Dyes made from coal tar are called aniline dyes.

Aniline dyes are far more common than any other dyes today. How strange it seems that many of the beautiful colors we see around us come from black, sticky coal tar that used to be thrown away as useless! (See COAL TAR; PHOENICIANS.)

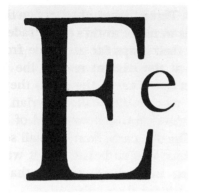

The letter E began as the picture of a man shouting for joy or praying (☖). In their alphabet the Phoenicians made the letter with straight lines (☖). The Greeks, after the alphabet came to them, turned it around and changed it somewhat (☖ ☖). The Romans made it as the later Greeks did (☖). It came down to us from the Romans without change.

In English e is used more often than any other letter in the alphabet. It stands for several sounds. It has a different sound in each of these words: *me, met, her, there.* In many words the e is silent. *Kite* and *tunnel* are two of them.

EAGLES In 1782 the United States Congress chose the bald eagle as the national emblem. It is pictured on the nation's coins and seals and medals. Choosing an eagle as a national emblem was not a new idea. Some 2,000 years earlier the Romans were using the eagle as a symbol of their power.

The bald eagle is not the only eagle found in the United States. There is also the golden eagle. The bald eagle has white feathers on its head. Its feet are bare. The golden eagle has a dark head and feathered feet. There are other eagles in other parts of the world.

Eagles are majestic birds. They may be over three feet long, and their wings may measure more than six feet from tip to tip.

As anyone would guess, eagles build big nests. These nests may be several feet across. Bald eagles usually place theirs in the tops of tall trees. Golden eagles nest on mountain crags and cliffs. Two or three eggs are laid in a nest. The young birds when hatched are covered with down. They can fly in about ten weeks.

Bald eagles eat mostly fish. Their good sight helps them to see fish from high in the air. They swoop down and catch the fish with their strong beaks and claws. They sometimes save themselves work by stealing fish other birds have caught.

Golden eagles eat mostly warm-blooded animals. They are wonderful hunters. As a rule they catch rabbits, gophers, and mice, but with their great strength they can carry away lambs and baby deer.

These great birds of prey are protected by law. Even so, they are becoming fewer. There is danger that they may disappear. (See BIRDS; BIRDS OF PREY.)

EARS Our ears make it possible for us to hear. Having two ears lets us know from what direction a sound is coming. Our ears also help us keep our balance.

A person's ear has three parts: the outer ear, the middle ear, and the inner ear. The outer ear is the part we see. It catches sound waves and sends them through a tube to the eardrum. The eardrum is a thin sheet of skin stretched tight. Just inside the eardrum, in the middle ear, are three tiny bones—the hammer, the anvil, and the stirrup. These little bones carry the sounds on to the inner ear. There nerves pick up the sound messages and carry them to the brain. The nerve endings are in a part of the ear shaped like a snail shell. Near by are three horseshoe-shaped tubes

Golden Eagle

Bald Eagle

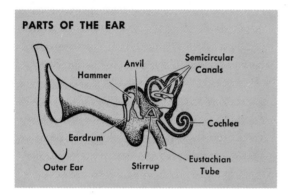

PARTS OF THE EAR

Hammer · Anvil · Semicircular Canals · Cochlea · Eardrum · Outer Ear · Stirrup · Eustachian Tube

filled with fluid. These tubes are called the semicircular canals. Our ears help us keep our balance by means of them.

The Eustachian (u STA ki an) tube leads from the middle ear to the throat. Air can reach the middle ear through it.

Many other animals have ears, but some of their ears are very different from ours. Birds have no outer ears. The openings into a bird's ears are hidden by feathers. The ears of frogs and toads show as big circles of skin just back of their eyes. Crickets are among the few insects with ears. Their ears are on their front legs.

Some animals can hear better than we do. Dogs, for instance, can hear sounds too high for us to hear. (See SOUND.)

EARTH The earth is one of the sun's family of planets. It travels around the sun just as all the other planets do. It takes the earth a year to make its journey around the sun. A year seems a long time for a journey. But the distance the earth travels is so great that, to cover it in a year, the earth must travel very fast—18 miles a second. This is over 1,000 miles a minute. If an airplane could travel as fast, it could fly across the United States from San Francisco to New York in less than three minutes.

The traveling of the earth around the sun helps cause the seasons. We have summer when the earth is at one place on its journey, and the other seasons when it is at other places.

As the earth travels around the sun, it spins like a top. It spins around an imaginary line which we call its axis. The North Pole is at one end of this axis. The South Pole is at the other. The spinning of the earth causes day and night.

The earth's axis is tilted. As it spins, the earth is like a top that is leaning a little to one side. The tilting of the axis also helps cause the seasons.

There is an imaginary circle around the earth halfway between the North and South Poles. It is called the equator. There is nothing on the earth to mark this halfway line. A person can cross it without knowing that he is doing so.

The earth is an almost perfect ball. It is a little flattened at the poles. It measures 24,902 miles at the equator. It measures 24,860 miles around through the poles. No place on the earth can be more than 12,451 miles from any place else.

The half of the earth north of the equator is the Northern Hemisphere. "Hemisphere" means "half a sphere." A sphere is

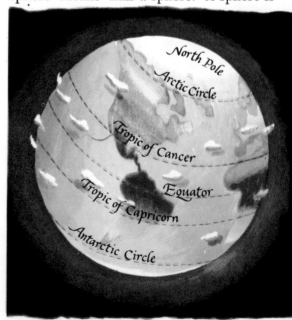

North Pole · Arctic Circle · Tropic of Cancer · Equator · Tropic of Capricorn · Antarctic Circle

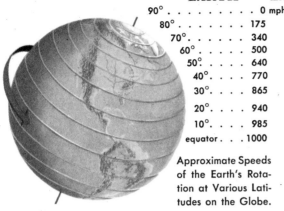

90°	0 mph
80°	175
70°	340
60°	500
50° . . .	640
40° . . .	770
30° . . .	865
20° . . .	940
10° . . .	985
equator . . .	1000

Approximate Speeds of the Earth's Rotation at Various Latitudes on the Globe.

a ball. The half of the earth south of the equator is the Southern Hemisphere.

The earth can be divided in halves in another way, too. The half with the Americas in it is the Western Hemisphere. The other half is the Eastern Hemisphere.

More than two-thirds of the earth's surface is covered with water. A globe can be turned so that almost nothing but the blue for oceans shows.

All around the earth there is a layer of air. This ocean of air is really as much a part of the earth as the oceans of water are. The chief reason we do not feel ourselves racing around the sun is that the earth carries its air along with it.

The earth is sometimes called a little planet of a little sun. It is true that four of the planets in our sun's family are much bigger than the earth. It is true, too, that our sun is one of the smaller suns, or stars. But no one yet knows of another planet in the universe where people like us could live. Perhaps there are many "earths" like ours circling around distant suns. But so far no one can be sure. (See PLANETS; SEASONS; SOLAR SYSTEM; STARS; SUN; UNIVERSE.)

EARTH HISTORY The earth is very old. Scientists think it is at least three billion years old, and it may be much older. In its long history it has changed in many ways.

There have been, for instance, changes in land and sea. Many parts of the earth that are now dry were once covered with water. In the same way, part of the floor of the sea was once dry land. The little map below shows North America as it was about 100 million years ago and as it is today. It would take many, many maps like this one to tell the whole story of how land and sea have changed.

The climate of the earth has also changed many times. There have been periods when large parts of the earth were covered with ice. At other times much of the earth was far warmer than it is now. The climate has changed from dry to wet and from wet to dry, too. Great forests once grew in places that are desert today.

Many people believe that mountains never change. But this idea is wrong. In the earth's long history there have been times of much mountain building. There have been other times when no new mountains were being made and when old ones were being worn away.

Some mountains are volcanoes. At times in the earth's history there have been many more volcanoes than there are now. Sometimes great floods of lava have poured out of long cracks in the earth's crust.

The living things on the earth have changed a great deal, too. For millions and millions of years all the plants and animals on the earth lived in the sea. Then land plants and animals appeared. Many kinds of plants and animals that once were common have long since disappeared. There was a time, for instance, when little

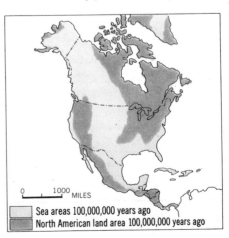

0 ___ 1000 MILES

☐ Sea areas 100,000,000 years ago
■ North American land area 100,000,000 years ago

animals called trilobites swarmed the sea-shores. There are now no trilobites. There was another time when giant reptiles called dinosaurs were very common. The dinosaurs, too, disappeared long ago.

Scientists have learned about the great changes in the earth's history by studying rocks. In many places the earth's crust is made up of layers of rock. The layers of rock tell a story to scientists just as the pages in a storybook do.

Scientists can read the story of the earth from its rocks partly because they know that different rocks are made in different ways. Some are made at the bottom of lakes and seas. Others are made from hot lava that pours from volcanoes. Still others are made from hot rock that cools deep underground. Scientists know, too, that some rocks have been greatly changed since they were first made. They know what brings these changes about.

Fossils help scientists read the story of the earth, too. Fossils are signs of living things of long ago found preserved in rocks. From fossils we know about the strange animals and plants that once lived on the earth. Fossils tell, too, about changes in climate and changes in land and sea.

Mountains can be made in different ways. The rock storybook tells how each mountain was made.

It would not be easy to read a storybook that had been thrown in a fire several times. It would not be easy to read a book that had some of its pages crumpled up. It would be even harder to read a book that had lost some of its pages. Reading the rock storybook is like reading a book with its pages scorched and crumpled and even torn out. For in places layers of rock have been covered with hot lava. In places they have been pushed out of shape and crumpled up. And in places they have been worn away by wind and water and ice. But even though the rock book is hard to read, scientists have been able to read a great deal of the story of the earth from it. The

chart tells a part of the earth's long story. This chart reads from the bottom upward.

In the beginning, there was a long, long time when there were no living things on the earth. Then came a time of very simple plants and animals. It was followed by the Age of Trilobites. Until the end of that age none of the animals on earth had backbones. The first animals with backbones were fishes. Fishes appeared long before there were any amphibians or reptiles or mammals or birds.

The Coal Age gets its name because most of our coal was made then. The coal was made from forests that grew in swamps. Amphibians appeared during the Coal Age.

After the Coal Age came the Age of Reptiles, and after that the Age of Mammals. Between one and two million years ago the great Ice Age began. Scientists think that people first appeared on the earth during the great Ice Age.

The time we live in now we can call the Age of Man. People, of course, are mammals. The Age of Man is, then, a part of the Age of Mammals. But people play a very different part in the history of the earth from the part played by earlier mammals. They are changing the earth in many ways to suit themselves. They dam streams to form lakes. They straighten rivers and shores. They dig canals and fill in swamps. They dig tunnels through mountains. Many of the changes made on the earth in recent years are man-made.

On the chart the common names for the different chapters in the earth's history are given. Some of the names scientists use are given, too. "Paleozoic (pa le o ZO ik) Era" is one of them. "Paleozoic" comes from Greek words meaning "ancient life."

Every chart of this kind tells the same story: The earth is very old, and its story is a story of great change. (See BIRDS OF YESTERDAY; COAL; DINOSAURS; FOSSILS; ICE AGE; LIFE THROUGH THE AGES; MAMMALS OF YESTERDAY; ROCKS; TRILOBITE.)

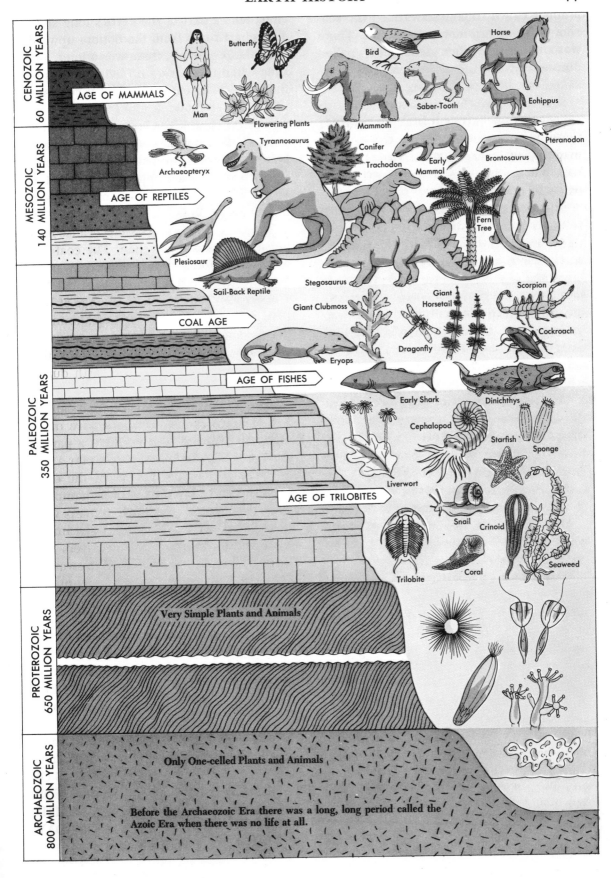

EARTHQUAKES Rather often, in one place or another, the land begins to shake. We say that there is an earthquake.

In an earthquake the earth may not shake very hard. The quake may do no damage. Perhaps it only rattles windows, or dishes on shelves, and frightens people a little. But an earthquake sometimes does an enormous amount of damage. It may shake down buildings. It may destroy a whole city and kill thousands of people. An earthquake out at sea may send great waves rushing in over seacoasts near by.

The worst earthquake in the history of the United States was in 1906. It almost ruined the city of San Francisco. It killed nearly 500 people and destroyed about $500,000,000 worth of property. Much of this damage was done, not by the quaking itself, but by fires that broke out as a result of the earthquake.

Another famous earthquake took place in Kansu Province in China in 1920. This earthquake covered 300 square miles and killed 200,000 people.

Sometimes an earthquake occurs in connection with a volcanic eruption. Just before a volcano erupted on one of the islands of Japan in 1914 there were more than 400 earthquakes on the island. Sometimes an earthquake is caused by the sliding of huge masses of rock along a great crack in the earth's crust. The San Francisco earthquake was caused in this way.

Places far away from mountains are rather safe from earthquakes. Earthquakes and mountain-building go together.

Scientists have invented an instrument that makes a record of earthquakes. It is called a seismograph. A seismograph can make a record of an earthquake thousands of miles away.

Engineers have learned how to build special kinds of houses in the places where earthquakes are likely to happen. These houses are able to shift slightly as the earth shakes, and so do not collapse. Reinforced concrete is a good material to use in building these houses. (See MOUNTAINS; VOLCANOES.)

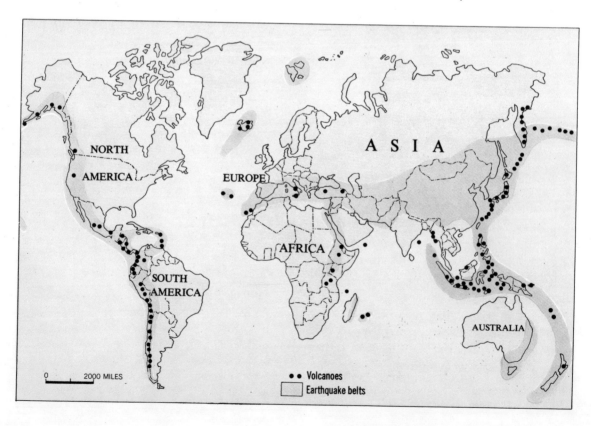

EARTHWORM As anyone can guess from their name, earthworms live in the ground. A hard rain may drive many of them up out of their burrows. But as soon as the rain is over, they go back again.

Earthworms have another common name. It is "angleworms." Fishermen often use these worms for bait.

An earthworm's soft body is made up of many "rings" called segments. There may be more than 100 segments in the body of a long worm.

Earthworms cannot live in very dry soil. For they drink through their skin. They breathe through their skin, too.

Robins eat many earthworms. But it is real work for a robin to pull an earthworm out of the ground. On the worm there are

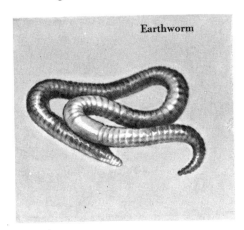

Earthworm

bristles that stick into the walls of its burrow. These bristles also help the worm crawl slowly along.

An earthworm actually eats its way through the ground. It makes a burrow and gets food at the same time. The food it gets from the soil is dead plant material. At night an earthworm may put its head out of its burrow to find bits of leaves. It pulls these back into its burrow to eat.

By digging burrows earthworms leave tiny holes which make it easy for air and water to get into the soil. Besides, they make soil finer by grinding it up in their gizzards. They make it richer, too. They are good friends of the farmer.

An angel sat at the empty tomb of Jesus.

EASTER The day we celebrate Christ's rising from the dead is called Easter. It always comes on Sunday, and the Sunday is always in either March or April. But without a calendar we cannot tell what Sunday Easter will be. The date depends on when the moon is full in those months. Easter can never be earlier than March 22. It can never be later than April 25.

To many people Easter means the coming of spring. In the spring trees send out new leaves. Bulbs that have rested in the ground all winter send up leaves and flowers. Moths come out of their cocoons. Birds build nests and lay their eggs. For hundreds of years eggs have been used to stand for the awakening of life in the spring. We color Easter eggs and give them to our friends as a way of saying, "Spring is here."

The blooming of lilies is a sign of Easter.

EAST INDIES The islands of the East Indies make up the largest group of islands in the world. They lie between Australia and southeastern Asia. There are five big islands in the group. The biggest, New Guinea, is the next-to-the-largest island in the whole world. Borneo is only a little smaller than New Guinea, and Sumatra is not far behind. There are several thousand smaller islands in the group. These islands cover an area of more than 1,000,000 square miles altogether.

It is hot the year round in the East Indies, and there is a great deal of rain. Much of the land on some of the islands is covered with jungle. There are many mountains. More than 100 of them are volcanoes, some of which are still active.

Not very long after a Portuguese explorer found a way around Africa to India, Dutch traders began sailing over that route to the Far East. They came to the East Indies and built trading posts there. Valuable tea and spices were shipped from the East Indies to Europe. A powerful Dutch trading company, the Dutch East India Company, succeeded in driving out British, French, Spanish, and Portuguese traders. Little by little the Dutch took possession of most of the land in the islands. The island territories the Dutch owned came to be called the Netherlands Indies.

After World War II all parts of the Netherlands Indies except New Guinea became independent. They now form the Republic of Indonesia. (See INDONESIA.)

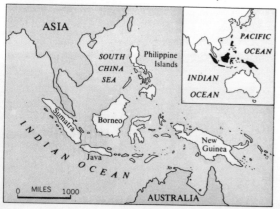

Testing an Echo

ECHO If a person shouts at a solid stone wall, his words often come back to him. He hears them as an echo.

Echoes occur when sound waves strike a hard, smooth surface and are bent back. Sound can be reflected from a wall just as light can be reflected from a mirror. A rough surface breaks up the sound waves.

In a valley where mountains are all around, a sound may be echoed many times. Some places are famous for their echoes. In one place in Ireland 100 echoes of a bugle note have been counted.

To experiment with echoes, a person should be at least 60 feet away from the wall he is sending the sound against. If he is any closer, the echo comes back so soon that it gets mixed up with the original sound. (See SOUND.)

ECLIPSES The moon does not give off any light of its own. It would not shine if the sun did not shine on it. Quite often— sometimes as often as three times in one year—the moon travels into the earth's shadow. With the earth shutting off the sunlight, the moon stops shining brightly. We say, when this happens, that there is a total eclipse of the moon.

Sometimes the moon travels across just one edge of the earth's shadow. Then only a part of the moon is darkened. We say that there is a partial eclipse.

Even during a total eclipse the moon does not completely disappear. The air around the earth bends some of the sun's rays so they strike the moon. Instead of disappearing, the moon looks dull red.

There cannot be an eclipse of the moon unless the moon is on the opposite side of the earth from the sun—when the moon is full. The moon cannot get into the earth's shadow at any other time.

There are eclipses of the sun, too. An eclipse of the sun occurs when the moon moves between the earth and the sun and shuts off the view of the sun from part of the earth. The moon is too small to ever hide the sun from the whole earth.

If the sun's entire disk is hidden by the moon, we say that there is a total eclipse. If only a part of the sun's disk is hidden, we say that there is a partial eclipse. There are always at least two eclipses of the sun in a year, and there may be as many as five. But most of the eclipses are only partial eclipses.

An eclipse of the sun does not last nearly as long as an eclipse of the moon. A total eclipse of the moon lasts for about two hours. A total eclipse of the sun never lasts for more than eight minutes.

During a total eclipse of the sun, the whole round disk of the sun is hidden. But the bright band of light around the sun— the "corona," it is called—still shows. So do some of the flames that shoot up from the sun. So much sunlight, however, is shut off that darkness falls just as if the

AN ECLIPSE OF THE SUN

sun had set. Chickens often go to roost, and other animals go to their barns. But in a very few minutes the "night" is over.

An eclipse of the moon can be seen from half the earth, but an eclipse of the sun can be seen only in the narrow path where the moon's shadow falls. Astronomers often make long trips to see a total eclipse of the sun. They are willing to go a long way because there are many problems about the sun and the stars that they can study best during a total eclipse.

People of long ago were frightened by eclipses. But today we are not afraid of them. Scientists now understand eclipses so well that they know all the eclipses there will be in the next several thousand years. (See ASTRONOMY; EARTH; MOON; SOLAR SYSTEM; SUN.)

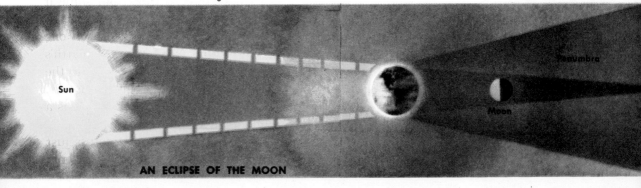

AN ECLIPSE OF THE MOON

Total population.......3,777,000
Area (square miles).....105,743

ELEVATION
Feet
Over 10000
5000 — 10000
2000 — 5000
1000 — 2000
0 — 1000

0   50 MILES

Coffee
Beef Cattle
Sugar
Cotton
Sheep
Textiles
Cocoa Beans
Potatoes

ECUADOR This small South American country was named Ecuador for a good reason. The equator crosses it. And the Spanish word for equator is *ecuador*.

The people of Ecuador speak Spanish. Some of them have only Spanish ancestors. But most people there are either Indian or part Spanish and part Indian. More than 400 years ago, Spaniards conquered the Indians living there. Spain ruled the land for about 300 years. But since 1830 Ecuador has been a free republic. It is as large as

Florida and Georgia together. Between 3 and 4 million people live in Ecuador.

The Andes Mountains run north and south through Ecuador. They are very high here. The land between them and the Pacific coast is low, wet, and always hot. So is the land east of them. And the mountains shut off eastern Ecuador from the coast.

About three-fourths of Ecuador's people live in its mountains. Nearly all the rest of the population live in the coastal lowland. Important crops in the mountain valleys are wheat and potatoes. Quito, the capital, is a highland city very near the equator. Even though it is near the equator, every day there is like a cool spring day.

Before Ecuador had railroads and airlines, its highland people were much shut off from the rest of the world. There were only mule and llama trains to carry loads between the high land and the low coast. Such travel was slow and hard.

The llama is an important animal in Ecuador.

Most things that Ecuador sells to other countries come from its coastal lowland. From forests there come vegetable ivory, kapok, and balsa wood. Sugar cane, bananas, coffee, and cacao are raised on plantations. From cacao beans, chocolate is made. Hats made in Ecuador from leaves of *jipijapa* palms, and called Panama hats, are worn in many lands. (See ANDES; INCAS; SOUTH AMERICA.)

Ecuador has sugar plantations and refineries.

THOMAS EDISON

EDISON, THOMAS ALVA (1847-1931) The man called "The Wizard of Menlo Park" was probably the world's greatest inventor. He invented many wonderful things. His name was Thomas Edison.

Edison's most famous invention was the incandescent electric lamp. In lamps of the kinds used before the days of electricity, something has to burn to make light. Kerosene is burned in a kerosene lamp, and gas is burned in a gas lamp. A candle gives off light when the wax in it burns. In an incandescent lamp something is heated white hot so that it glows. It does not burn up—at least, not for a long time.

Around the year 1879 many men were trying to make a good incandescent lamp. Three things were necessary. One was a way to heat the material until it glowed. Electricity does this easily when the material is in the form of a fine thread, called a filament. Another was a way to keep air away so that the filament would not burn. Edison solved this problem by sealing the filament in a glass bulb from which he pumped out the air. The third was Edison's biggest problem—a kind of filament which would glow white hot for a long time.

By the time Edison began working on his incandescent lamp, he was already a successful inventor with a staff of assistants. He sent some of his men far and wide to bring back material for filaments to his laboratory in Menlo Park, N. J.

Of the thousands of different filaments he tested, those made of carbon were found to be best. Carbon filaments were made by charring wood fibers, and some wood fibers worked better than others. Another long search was made. Finally a certain kind of bamboo fiber was found that seemed good. On October 21, 1879, Edison's first lamp made with a charred bamboo filament was ready to be tested.

The lamp was switched on. It glowed with a beautiful soft light. Breathlessly Edison and his helpers watched to see how long it would glow. Hour after hour they watched. No one wanted to sleep. They watched for two whole days and nights, and the lamp still glowed on. It was a success.

Since then incandescent lamps have been greatly improved. After Edison showed that such lamps could be made, many people became interested in trying to make better ones.

Edison was born in Milan, Ohio. He did not like school, but he enjoyed being taught at home by his mother. He also liked to learn things by himself by reading and experimenting. He had a laboratory in the basement of his home.

Edison started to earn money when he was very young. He wanted to buy for himself what he needed for his experiments.

Before he was 15 he published a newspaper which he called the *Weekly Herald*. His printing office was set up in the baggage car of a train on which he worked.

One day Edison saved the life of a little boy. The boy's father rewarded Edison by teaching him how to be a telegraph operator. As a telegraph operator Edison found ways to improve the methods of sending messages by telegraph.

Edison's inventions number well over 1,000. Important among them, in addition to the incandescent lamp, are motion pictures, the phonograph, the multiplex telegraph, the carbon telephone transmitter, and the microphone. All of us owe a great deal to this famous inventor.

Court Scene

Lyre

Headdress

Mirror

These relics—about 3,500 years old—were found in an Egyptian tomb.

Charm

Razor

Necklace

Scarab Bracelet

EGYPT The lands near the eastern end of the Mediterranean Sea are often called the "cradle of civilization." Egypt is one of them. It is a desert land in the northeast corner of Africa. The narrow, fertile valley of the great Nile River cuts through it. For centuries desert and sea set Egypt apart from the wars of its neighbors and kept it safe from invasion.

Good hunting and fishing along the banks of the Nile attracted wandering tribesmen. They settled there and in time became farmers. They grew patches of barley, wheat, legumes, vegetables, and flax. The flax they wove into linen on simple looms. They raised sheep, donkeys, cattle, pigs, and goats. The great Nile furnished water. It furnished new, rich soil every summer when it flooded its banks.

The Egyptians worked hard, and as the centuries went by they made great strides upward. They invented ways to carry Nile waters farther back and higher up on the banks. They learned to make tools and hunting weapons out of copper. They learned to make plows and to harness oxen to them. And, perhaps more important, they learned to write. Egyptian writing was a rebus-like picture writing called hieroglyphics. At first it was done on stone and clay, but later much of it was done on papyrus, a kind of paper made from papyrus plants that grew along the Nile.

People have learned a great deal about the Egyptians from their writing. They have learned a great deal, too, from objects buried with them in their tombs and from pictures they carved and painted on tomb and temple walls. The dry climate of Egypt has preserved many of these ancient records. The pictures show Egyptians plowing their fields and harvesting their crops. They show them fishing with nets from reed boats on the Nile. They show trading boats traveling up the Nile with sails set to catch the wind.

As wandering hunters, Egyptians lived in tribes ruled by chiefs. But as farmers they gradually developed small states ruled by "little kings." About 5,000 years ago all the little kingdoms of Egypt were united into one nation.

A long line, or dynasty, of strong kings called pharaohs began to rule this united Egypt. Their capital city was Memphis. Early in the reign of the pharaohs learned men worked out the first 365-day calendar so that accurate records could be kept of government affairs. The calendar we use today is much like the one the Egyptians invented nearly 5,000 years ago.

For nearly 2,000 years Egypt prospered. The pharaohs and their officers directed the work of irrigation. Farms produced more wheat than Egypt needed. The pharaohs sent men to mine copper, to quarry stone for palaces and temples, and to mine gold and turquoise. Traders traveled to neighboring countries and sold grain, linen, and articles of copper. They bought timber, ivory, lapis lazuli, and olive oil.

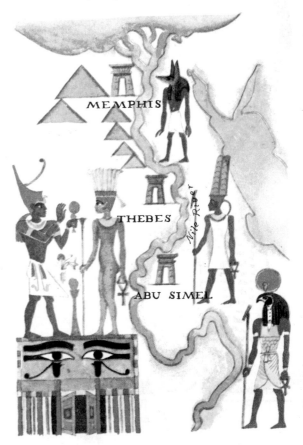

MEMPHIS

THEBES

Nile River

ABU SIMEL

The famous pyramids are at Giza, near Cairo.

Religion played an important part in the lives of the people. They believed that the pharaoh was a god and that when he died he rode the bright heavens with the great sun-god Re (RAY). The Egyptians worshiped many gods, and made up myths to explain many of the things they did not understand in nature.

The Egyptians believed in a life after death that was like the life they knew in Egypt. They made their dead into mummies and buried with them all the things they would need in the next world—food and clothing, pottery and furniture, weapons, and ornaments. The pharaohs prepared great burial tombs for themselves. At Giza, near Memphis, pyramid tombs built by early pharaohs over 4,000 years ago still stand. They are one of the Seven Wonders of the Ancient World. Near them is the Sphinx, a great temple-monument carved during the Pyramid Age.

In time a warrior pharaoh, Thutmose III, led his armies into Asia over the trading-caravan trails. He conquered many of the nearby peoples of Asia. Earlier pharaohs had already conquered peoples of the south. Egypt became the richest, most powerful empire of the day.

Thebes, then the capital city, was magnificent with huge statues and great stone temples built by thousands of slaves. The famous Hall of Karnak was one of the temples. Far to the south, at Abu Simbel in Nubia, giant statues of a famous pharaoh, Ramses II, have towered over the Nile for 3,200 years.

During the empire some subject peoples in Asia borrowed a few of the hundreds of hieroglyphic signs in Egyptian writing and worked out a way to write with just those few signs. It was the first alphabet. The Egyptians, however, kept their old, complicated way of writing.

Egypt could not hold the empire its pharaohs had built. Some of the conquered peoples broke away. The time came when Egypt could not keep out invading armies. In the seventh century B.C. it fell before warring Assyrians. And in less than 100 years the Persians came to conquer and named their leader pharaoh of Egypt. Later other conquerors came. There were Greeks, Romans, Arabs, French, and British.

In 1922 Egypt became a free nation once again when it was granted its independence by Great Britain. On Feb. 1, 1958, Egypt joined Syria and became part of a single nation—the United Arab Republic.

Today a green ribbon of farmland still stretches along the Nile and spreads fanwise over the delta land near the Mediterranean Sea. Most of the Egyptians are still farmers in tiny villages. But they have a new crop—fine, silky cotton—to sell to many foreign countries. They now irrigate more farmland than ever before, for modern dams across the Nile store much water for use when the river is low.

The delta of the Nile is now crisscrossed by canals and railway lines. At Cairo (KI ro) these delta routes meet the long river route. Cairo is now the capital and a great commercial city. It is the largest city of Africa. Many tourists go to Egypt to see the pyramids and other records of its past. Standing near old tombs and temples, they may hear a whirring in the bright sky. It may be a helicopter dusting the cotton crop or a great air liner bound for Cairo.

Egypt was a "gift of the Nile." But Egypt's greatness was due also to its inventive people. (See ALPHABET; MUMMIES; NILE RIVER; OBELISK; PAPYRUS; PYRAMIDS; SUEZ CANAL.)

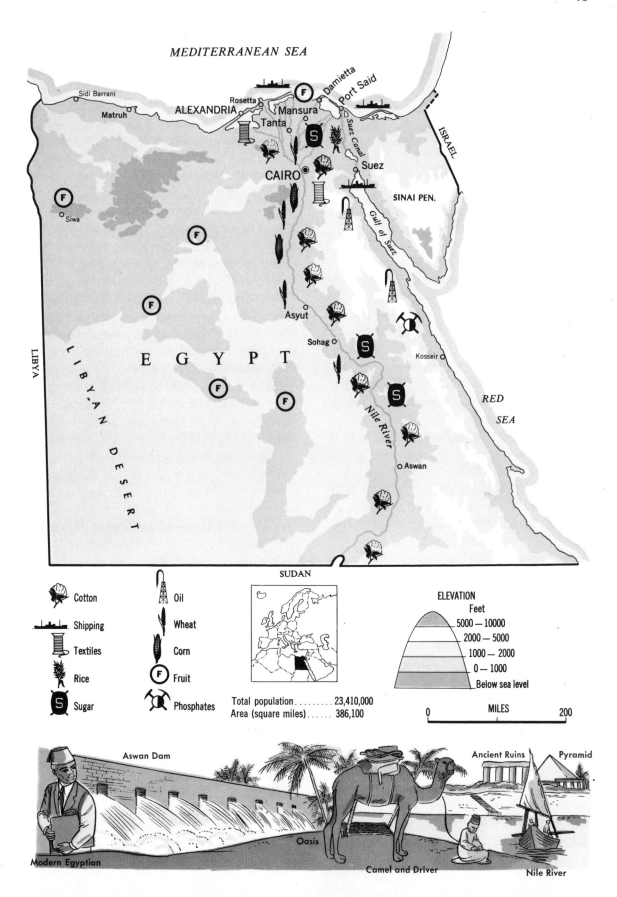

MEDITERRANEAN SEA

Sidi Barrani
Matruh
ALEXANDRIA
Rosetta
Damietta
Port Said
Mansura
Tanta
CAIRO
Suez Canal
Suez
ISRAEL
SINAI PEN.
Gulf of Suez
Siwa
LIBYA
L I B Y A N   D E S E R T
E G Y P T
Asyut
Sohag
Kosseir
RED SEA
Nile River
Aswan
SUDAN

Legend

Cotton
Shipping
Textiles
Rice
Sugar
Oil
Wheat
Corn
Fruit
Phosphates

Total population 23,410,000
Area (square miles) 386,100

ELEVATION
Feet
5000 — 10000
2000 — 5000
1000 — 2000
0 — 1000
Below sea level

0   MILES   200

Modern Egyptian
Aswan Dam
Oasis
Camel and Driver
Ancient Ruins
Pyramid
Nile River

Eiffel Tower

EIFFEL TOWER There was a world's fair in Paris in 1889. For it Alexandre Gustave Eiffel built a high tower. The tower was named for him. When the fair ended, Eiffel Tower was left standing. Some of the people of Paris think that it should be torn down because it is not beautiful. But it is so famous and so many people visit it every year that it will probably be left standing for many years more.

The tower is 984 feet tall. At the time it was built, it was taller than anything else anyone had ever made. But 41 years later, in New York, a skyscraper was built that was taller. It was the Chrysler Building. Now the Empire State Building is nearly 300 feet higher than Eiffel Tower.

Eiffel Tower has three "floors" and, near the top, a balcony. From the balcony one can see more than 50 miles. Some of the visitors who climb to the balcony get seasick because the tower sways in the wind.

Since the tower is made of iron, it must be painted to keep it from rusting. But painting it is not easy. It takes so long that the painters are always at work on it. By the time they get to where they started, they have to begin over again.

The tower has proved useful for other things besides sight-seeing. It is used as a weather station. And for years wireless and radio messages have been sent from it. Now it is also used to transmit television programs. (See PARIS.)

EINSTEIN, ALBERT (1878-1955) Scientists around the world are finding more and more proof of many of the very complicated ideas of Albert Einstein. These ideas are an attempt to explain the whole universe. They helped make possible such things as television and the atomic bomb.

Einstein was born in Ulm, Germany. When he was a year old, his family moved to Munich. Einstein later went to school there. He did very well in mathematics, but not in other subjects. At 15, he failed an examination to attend a university in Zurich, Switzerland. After another year of study he passed the examination.

In 1905, when Einstein was only 26, four of his articles appeared in a German magazine. These articles set forth some of his important ideas, among them his Theory of Relativity. The ideas in these articles made him immediately famous.

Einstein also became famous as a great believer in freedom. In 1933, after Hitler came to power in Germany, Einstein went to live in the United States. He continued his important studies there.

There are many stories of Einstein's kindness to others. In 1952 a young girl in Los Angeles wrote asking him how to solve one of her arithmetic problems. Einstein took the time to send her a careful answer. (See GENIUS; PHYSICS.)

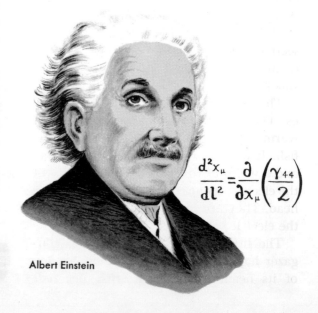

$$\frac{d^2 x_\mu}{dl^2} = \frac{\partial}{\partial x_\mu}\left(\frac{\gamma_{44}}{2}\right)$$

Albert Einstein

The electric eel is one of the most feared fishes.

ELECTRIC FISHES About 50 kinds of fishes give electric shocks to animals that come in contact with them. These fishes are called electric fishes. The shocks they give help them to get food and to protect themselves from their enemies.

The electric eel is a well-known electric fish. This fish is not really an eel. It gets its name because it is slender like an eel. Many electric eels grow to a length of eight feet and a weight of 50 pounds. Electric eels are found in the Amazon and Orinoco rivers in South America.

The electric batteries, or shocking organs, are along both sides of the eel. The shock they give is said to be strong enough to stun a horse. It is the most powerful shock found among the electric fishes. Each battery is made up of tiny six-sided sections. Nerves run from these sections to the brain. If these nerves are cut, no shock is given.

The rays are broad, much-flattened fishes. The electric ray, or torpedo, found in warm seas is another well-known electric fish. It may grow to a length of five feet and a width of three feet. The batteries of the electric ray are on the sides of the fish's head. They are much like the batteries of the electric eel.

The little electric fish called the stargazer has its shocking organs on the top of its head. A stargazer often lies half buried in the sand and waits for some small animal to come along. The electric shock the small animal gets when it touches the stargazer paralyzes it and makes it easy eating for the fish. The stargazers are seldom more than a foot long. Like the torpedoes, they are found in warm seas.

The electric catfish, which grows to be about three feet long, is found in fresh water in Africa. This fish gives a powerful shock, almost as strong as the shock of the electric eel. But its shocking organs are quite different from those of the eel. They form a kind of greasy layer just under the skin. The fish can give off a number of very short shocks. Then it must eat and rest before it can continue its shocking habit. This fish has been found in Egyptian pictures that are more than 4,000 years old. (See FISHES.)

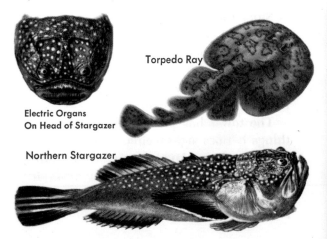

Torpedo Ray

Electric Organs
On Head of Stargazer

Northern Stargazer

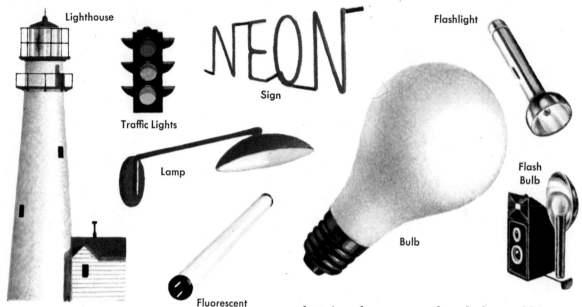

Lighthouse

Traffic Lights

NEON Sign

Lamp

Fluorescent Tube

Bulb

Flashlight

Flash Bulb

ELECTRICITY FOR LIGHT

ELECTRICITY In a huge sign in one of our cities, electric lights spell out the words "Electricity Your Servant." Electricity *is* the servant of many millions of people.

The pictures on these two pages and the next two remind us of some of the ways in which electricity helps us. But electricity helps us in still other ways. The pictures do not show, for instance, big loads of iron being lifted by an electromagnet, an X-ray picture being taken, or knives and forks and spoons being plated with silver. Electricity is a true Jack-of-all-trades.

Electricity has not been a servant for much more than 100 years, but it has been known since the days of the ancient Greeks. The word "electricity" comes from the Greek word for amber. The Greeks discovered that, if a piece of amber was rubbed with fur, it would pick up bits of straw or other lightweight materials. Later scientists discovered that other materials would act like amber. They could be given charges of electricity. Small sparks of electricity could be drawn from them. Today getting a charge of electricity by shuffling across a thick rug on a winter day is a common stunt. There are toys that are worked by electric charges produced by rubbing. Charges of this kind are called charges of frictional, or static, electricity. They are not very useful.

Before electricity could become a good servant, some way had to be found of getting a steadily flowing current of electricity. Scientists found ways of getting currents of electricity before they had any idea of what a current of electricity is. Now, although no one can see a current of electricity, scientists can tell us a great deal about it. To understand their explanation we have to know something about atoms.

All substances are made up of tiny particles called atoms. Atoms in turn are made up of very, very tiny particles called electrons. The electrons whirl around centers, or nuclei, made up of other particles—protons and neutrons. Protons and neutrons stay in their atoms, but electrons, when given enough push, can hop from atom to atom. An electric current is a stream of electrons moving through a material.

Knowing about electrons helps us understand charges of frictional electricity, too. When two substances are rubbed together, electrons may be rubbed off one substance on to the other. Having either more electrons than usual or fewer than usual gives an object a charge of electricity.

More than 150 years ago an Italian scientist named Volta found a way of getting an electric current. He invented an electric cell. But only a weak current came from it. Better cells were made and stronger currents could be got from them. But electricity became truly useful after Michael Faraday invented a machine to push electrons on their way. A machine which furnishes a current of electricity is called a generator. Today we use both cells and generators.

A battery is made up of two or more electric cells joined together. We use batteries in such things as portable radios, flashlights, hearing aids, electric games, and automobiles. The current which comes into our houses, stores, and offices and lights

Room Heater

Heating Pad   Coffee Pot

Iron

our streets and runs big machines in factories comes from generators.

Many batteries are made up of dry cells. An ordinary dry cell has a carbon rod in the center, a zinc can on the outside, and a moist mixture of chemicals between the carbon and the zinc. A dry cell is not truly dry, but there is no liquid that can spill. The action of the chemicals on the zinc starts the flow of electrons.

A storage battery is made up of wet cells. Each one has in it plates of lead, plates of lead peroxide, and a mixture of water and acid. A storage battery gets its name because, to keep it in working order, a cur-

rent of electricity from a generator is sent through it from time to time. In a sense the battery stores up the current from the generator. Sending a current through a storage battery is called charging the battery.

A generator is made up of magnets and coils of wire. Either the coils of wire or the magnets must be whirled round and round to make a generator produce a current. Some generators are driven by great water wheels. There are many electric power plants at waterfalls and dams. Other generators are driven by steam turbines. A house current may come from a power plant next door. It may come instead from a power plant at a waterfall that is more than 100 miles away.

Using electricity means more than having something to furnish a current and something for the current to run. Circuits, or paths, for the current must be set up. And there must be easy ways of starting and stopping the current.

ELECTRICITY FOR HEAT

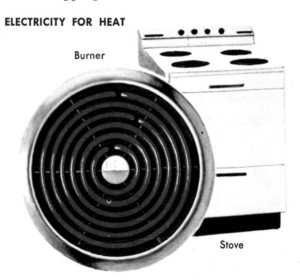

Burner

Stove

To set up an electric circuit a person has to know that a current flows through some materials much more easily than through others. Substances it flows through easily are called good conductors. Substances that it does not flow through easily are called poor conductors. Poor conductors are just as important as good conductors in making a current of electricity go where

Clothes Washer

Clock

Trolley

Vacuum
Cleaner

Motor

Fan

ELECTRICITY FOR MOTORS

we want it to go. The good conductors give it a roadway. The poor conductors keep it from straying off the roadway and going where it is not wanted. They prevent what we call short circuits. A short circuit is an easier path than the one we want the current to take.

A person must know, too, that a current will not flow unless there is a complete path from a battery or a generator back to the battery or generator. To stop a current from flowing we simply have to break the path somewhere. To start it we simply "mend" the break. Switches of many kinds can be used to make and break a circuit.

Usually most of the work of setting up a circuit is done for us. Wires bring current to our homes from power plants. Wires in the walls go to light sockets and electric stoves and wall plates, or receptacles. With electric stoves and lamps all we have to do is to switch on the current. Many electric appliances have cords made up of two wires with a plug at the end. The plug is pushed into a wall receptacle. Plugging in the cord joins the two wires of the appliance with two wires leading from outside to the receptacle. There is almost sure to be a switch on the appliance or the cord.

But when a person is experimenting, as the boy in the picture is doing, he must know how to set up a circuit. In the picture

a dry cell is furnishing the current for an electric bell. A push button is the device for making and breaking the circuit.

In the push button there are two metal connections. A wire from the cell is fastened to one connection. A wire from the bell is fastened to the other. There is a gap in the circuit until the boy pushes down the button of the push button and in doing so pushes down a piece of metal that links the two connections.

The wire the boy is using is copper, as most wire for electric circuits is. Copper is an excellent conductor of electricity and is fairly cheap. The wire is insulated— wrapped in a poor conductor of electricity. But at the ends of the pieces of wires, where the connections are made, the insulation has been removed.

Sometimes all the lights in a room go out when no one has touched the switch. Usually what has happened is that a fuse has "blown." Fuses are the watchmen that help keep our servant electricity from doing harm by producing unwanted heat. At times for some reason so much current may flow through the wires in a house that the wires begin to get hot. The heated wires could easily set fire to the walls. But the current also has to flow through the fuse. A fuse contains a piece of metal that melts rather easily. When too much current flows

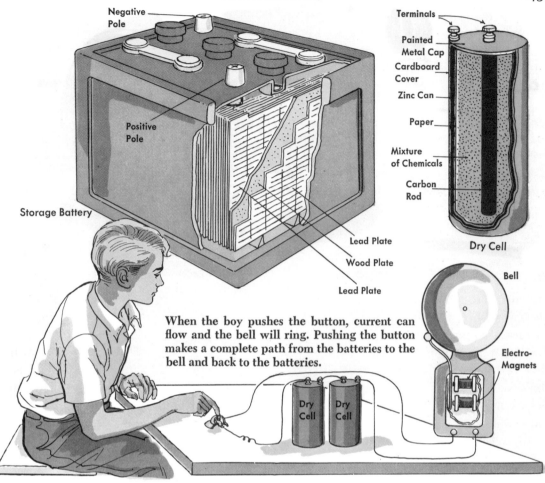

Negative Pole

Positive Pole

Storage Battery

Terminals

Painted Metal Cap

Cardboard Cover

Zinc Can

Paper

Mixture of Chemicals

Carbon Rod

Dry Cell

Lead Plate

Wood Plate

Lead Plate

Bell

Electro-Magnets

When the boy pushes the button, current can flow and the bell will ring. Pushing the button makes a complete path from the batteries to the bell and back to the batteries.

Dry Cell

Dry Cell

ELECTRICITY FOR SENDING MESSAGES

Television

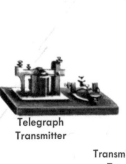

Telegraph Transmitter

Transmitting Tower

Telephone

Dictating Machine

Radio

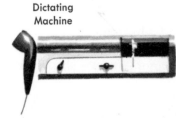

through the wires, the piece of metal in the fuse melts and breaks the circuit. Fuses blow most often because there is a short circuit or because too many appliances are being used at one time.

In buying and using electrical appliances there are some terms everyone needs to know. "Volt" is one. "Ampere" is another. "Watt" is a third.

The push that forces a current through a circuit is measured in volts. A dry cell has a push of only about 1½ volts. Most household appliances are built for a voltage of either 110 or 220.

An ampere is a measure of the strength of a current. Fuses are always marked in amperes. The marking shows how strong a current can flow through the fuse without making it blow.

Electric lamp bulbs are marked in watts. A 100-watt lamp gives a much brighter light than a 25-watt lamp. A watt is a measure of the amount of electricity an appliance uses. A kilowatt is 1,000 watts.

The current flows through a meter as it comes into our houses. The meter measures the electric power used. From its readings bills for electricity are figured. We find out how much we must pay for the help of this servant. (See ATOMS; EDISON, THOMAS; ENERGY; FARADAY, MICHAEL; INVENTIONS; LAMPS AND LIGHTING; MACHINERY; TELEGRAPH; TELEPHONE; TELEVISION.)

ELECTRONICS In 1913 an American inventor was tried in the courts in New York for getting money through the mails for shares in a worthless invention. The jury decided that he was not guilty, but the judge gave him a harsh lecture. He told the inventor to "get a common garden variety of job and stick to it." The inventor was Lee De Forest. The invention was the audion tube, which proved to be one of the greatest inventions of the 20th century. Like most inventions, the audion tube was based on earlier discoveries and inventions.

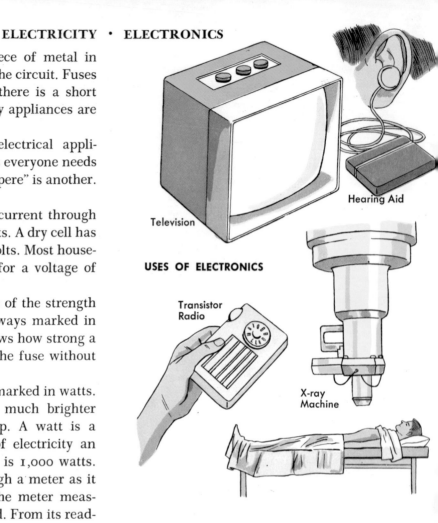

Television

Hearing Aid

USES OF ELECTRONICS

Transistor Radio

X-ray Machine

But De Forest added important ideas of his own. The use of the new tube in radio can be called the start of the electronic age we are in now.

Electron tubes more or less like De Forest's audion tube are used today not only in radio but also in television, radar, and the long-distance telephone. They are a part of the great calculating machines called "electronic brains" and of the electron microscope. They help doctors diagnose and treat diseases. They help make sound motion pictures and records. They make guided missiles possible. In mills and factories they have many uses.

Electricity was doing wonderful things before the days of electronics. Electric currents were carrying messages by telephone and telegraph. They were lighting streets and buildings, driving machines of many kinds, plating cheap metals with expen-

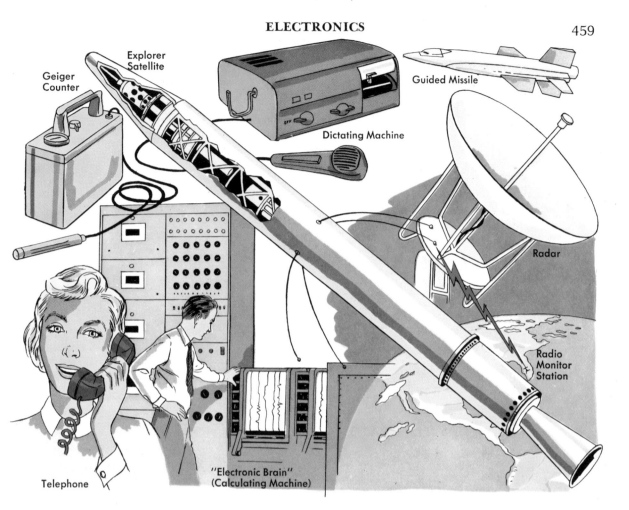

Geiger Counter

Explorer Satellite

Dictating Machine

Guided Missile

Radar

Radio Monitor Station

Telephone

"Electronic Brain" (Calculating Machine)

sive ones, making great lifting magnets work, operating heating devices, and making life easier in still other ways. It did not seem that there was much more for it to do. Then the whole new field of electronics was opened up.

The name "electronics" comes from the word "electron." Electrons are tiny electric particles. Every atom of every material is made up partly of electrons. In an electric current electrons move through solids or liquids. They "hop" from atom to atom. In electron tubes electrons move through a rare gas or through a vacuum. The electrons are driven out of some metals. Since they are driven away from atoms, they are called free electrons.

There are several ways of driving out the electrons. In radio tubes, heat is used. In the "electric eye" a sensitive metal plate gives out electrons when light rays fall on

it. In the picture tube in a television set, high voltage frees the electrons.

Some electron tubes are smaller than a peanut. But picture tubes in television sets may be more than two feet across.

In some electronic devices transistors are now taking the place of tubes. Transistors are made of crystals of germanium.

There seems to be no limit to what can be done with electronics. It promises to unlock many secrets for us. With its help telescopes will be able to see more of what is "out of sight," hidden flaws in materials will be found, and the floor of the sea can be explored without going beneath the water. We are already able to get word from the man-made moons that have been set to traveling around the earth. So much lies ahead for electronics that it is a promising field for the youth of today. (See RADIO; TELEVISION; TRANSISTOR.)

TABLE OF ELEMENTS

Element	Symbol
*Aluminum	Al
Americium	Am
Argon	A
Arsenic	As
Berkelium	Bk
Boron	B
Bromine	Br
*Calcium	Ca
Californium	Cf
†Carbon	C
Chlorine	Cl
Chromium	Cr
Cobalt	Co
Copper	Cu
Curium	Cm
Fluorine	F
Gold	Au
Helium	He
†Hydrogen	H
Iodine	I
Iridium	Ir
*Iron	Fe
Krypton	Kr
Lead	Pb
Lithium	Li
*Magnesium	Mg
Manganese	Mn
Mercury	Hg
Molybdenum	Mo
Neon	Ne
Neptunium	Np
Nickel	Ni
†Nitrogen	N
†*Oxygen	O
Phosphorus	P
Platinum	Pt
Plutonium	Pu
*Potassium	K
Radium	Ra
Selenium	Se
*Silicon	Si
Silver	Ag
*Sodium	Na
Sulfur	S
Tin	Sn
Titanium	Ti
Tungsten	W
Uranium	U
Vanadium	V
Zinc	Zn

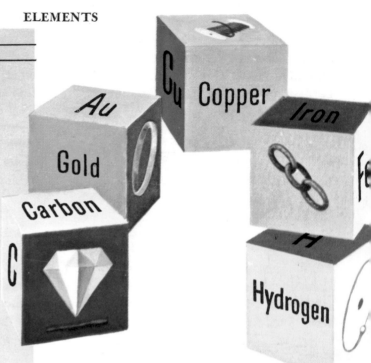

ELEMENTS The ancient Greeks had the idea that everything on earth was made up of four simple substances—fire, air, earth, and water. A part of their idea was right. All the millions of different materials in the world are made of certain simple substances. We call them elements. They can be thought of as the building blocks of the universe. But the Greeks were wrong about what the simple substances are and how many there are.

There are a few more than 100 elements. For many years scientists felt sure that there were just 92. There *are* just 92 natural elements. But scientists have produced several others in their laboratories.

More than three-fourths of all the elements are solids. Most of the others are gases. Carbon and iron are examples of solid elements. Oxygen and chlorine are gases. There are only two liquid elements. They are mercury and bromine.

The chart names 50 of the elements. It also gives the scientists' way of writing the name of each element—its symbol.

The symbols for most elements are easy to understand. It is easy to see why C was chosen to stand for carbon and O for oxygen. But it is not easy to see why Fe stands for iron and Au for gold. These symbols and others like them were made from the Latin names of the elements they stand for. *Ferrum* is the Latin word for iron. *Aurum* is the Latin word for gold.

In the chart the names of some elements are underlined. These are elements that have been produced in laboratories.

The materials of our bodies are made up of elements just as all other materials are. In the chart the four commonest elements in our bodies are marked with daggers.

The elements marked with a star on the chart are the eight commonest elements in the earth's crust. Oxygen is the most abundant of these. Silicon comes second.

The story of chemistry is partly a story of the discovery of one element after another. Many scientists made themselves famous by discovering an element. The English scientist Priestley, for example, is famous for his discovery of oxygen. Many elements were hard to discover for they are never found free. They are always, that is, joined with other elements.

One element, helium, was found in the sun before it was found on earth. Its name comes from the Greek word for sun. Scientists discovered it by studying sunlight. It is no wonder that helium was found first in the sun. It is rather rare on earth, while almost half the sun is made up of it. Almost all the rest of the sun is hydrogen. Other elements make up only about one one-hundredth of the sun.

The same story is true of the whole universe. The many billions of stars are mostly hydrogen and helium. There is 99 times as much hydrogen and helium in the universe as of all the other elements put together. (See CHEMISTRY.)

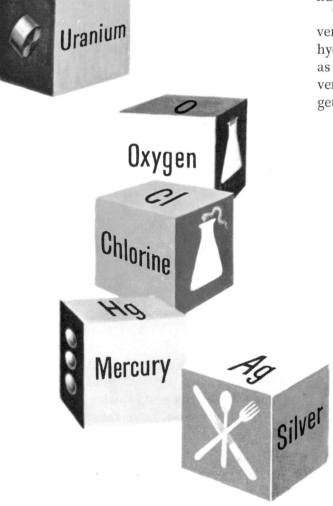

AFRICAN ELEPHANT

Elephants feed on grass and roots.

ELEPHANTS Of all the animals that live on land today, the elephant is the biggest. Jumbo, a famous circus elephant, was 11 feet tall and weighed six and a half tons. Elephants are strong, too. In circuses they often help push heavy wagons.

Jumbo was an African elephant, but most of the elephants in circuses and zoos are Indian elephants. Indian elephants are also called Asiatic elephants. African elephants have much bigger ears than Asiatic elephants. In Africa there are also pygmy elephants. "Pygmy" means "dwarf," but pygmy elephants are not really small. They are just small for elephants.

Asiatic elephants are more easily trained than African elephants. In Asia people have for years used elephants for working and hunting. Rulers there have been proud of their elephants. Royal elephants often have beautiful trappings.

An elephant's trunk is really its nose and upper lip, but the elephant uses it as a kind of hand. With it the elephant puts food in its mouth and sprays water on its back.

Elephants are plant eaters. They gather grass with their trunks and dig up roots with their sharp tusks. A circus elephant eats about 150 pounds of hay and drinks 50 gallons of water a day. (See CIRCUS; WHITE ELEPHANT.)

Indian Elephants

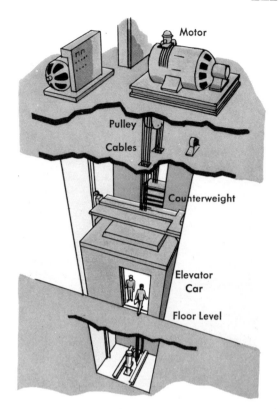

ELEVATOR No one would ever want an office high in a skyscraper if he had to climb flights of stairs to reach it. No skyscrapers were built until after elevators were invented. The Empire State Building is the world's tallest skyscraper. It has several miles of elevator shafts.

An elevator is a car that can be moved up and down a shaft from one floor to another. The car has cables fastened to it at the top. These cables go over pulleys at the top of the shaft. To the other end of these cables a weight is fastened. This weight weighs about as much as the elevator car and is called a "counterweight." The counterweight makes it easier to lift the car. A person waiting for an elevator often sees the counterweight move past. As the elevator goes up, the counterweight moves down. When the elevator goes down, the counterweight moves up.

The earliest elevators were hydraulic. They were pushed up by water. Now most elevators are run by low-speed electric motors that operate the pulleys.

Some elevators are automatic. The rider simply pushes a button as he enters the car, and the car goes to the floor he wants.

If an elevator were to fall several floors, any people in it might be badly hurt. But there are special safety brakes to keep an elevator from falling.

Escalators, or moving stairways, are taking the place of elevators in some buildings. They take up more room than elevators and are not so fast. They are not likely to take the place of elevators in tall skyscrapers.

ELEVATOR, GRAIN In the parts of the United States and Canada where much grain is raised, grain elevators, or granaries, are a common sight. Almost every village has one. Some cities have many.

A grain elevator is always tall. It is made mostly of big storage bins. Such an elevator gets its name because the grain has to be raised, or elevated, to the tops of the bins. The grain may be raised by an endless chain of buckets, or it may be sucked up through a big tube.

Grain spoils quickly if it is damp when it is stored. At the top of an elevator there are machines for drying damp grain. There are also machines for cleaning grain and scales for weighing it.

Elevators are a big help to farmers. The farmers can take their grain to the elevators as soon as it has been harvested. They do not have to store it on their farms. A big elevator like the one in the picture has room in its bins to store many millions of bushels of grain.

This elevator can hold millions of bushels of grain.

ELIZABETH I (1533-1603) Among England's past rulers are two famous queens—Elizabeth I and Victoria. The earlier of these queens, Elizabeth I, reigned during a most exciting time. America had been discovered not long before, and a whole New World was waiting to be explored.

Elizabeth I was 25 years old when she became queen. England was then poor. The people were quarreling among themselves about religion and many other things. The country had no friends among the other nations. There was even danger that France would conquer England.

But Elizabeth I proved to be a strong ruler. She was interested in everything new. Soon her seamen were going on daring voyages to explore the New World. Sir Walter Raleigh and Sir Francis Drake were two of the most famous explorers. English ships went out to trade with countries in all parts of the Old World, too. Never before had the English flag been seen in so many faraway places.

The Queen brought an end to the trouble with France. Later, in 1588, King Philip II

Elizabeth I reigned during a period of great exploration.

of Spain sent his powerful fleet, the Spanish Armada, to conquer England. Elizabeth's seamen won a great victory.

The most famous Englishman of Elizabeth's time was not an explorer or a fighter. He was a poet and writer of plays—William Shakespeare. There were many other great English writers at that time, too.

One of the first great English scientists also lived during Elizabeth's reign. He was Sir William Gilbert, who made many discoveries about magnets.

Although she sent her seamen all over the world, Elizabeth herself did almost no traveling. One of the longest journeys she ever took was from London to another English city, Bristol. It was only a little more than 100 miles, but she thought that it was

long and hard. She was thankful that she came through it safely.

Elizabeth was not always kind or fair. She imprisoned and even beheaded some of the people who did not agree with her. But she did so much to make England great that she was known as "Good Queen Bess."

For almost 400 years this famous queen was called simply Queen Elizabeth. Today she is called Elizabeth I, for another Elizabeth became queen of England in 1952. (See ARMADA; ENGLAND'S HISTORY.)

Lincoln's proclamation meant the end of slavery.

EMANCIPATION PROCLAMATION
In 1861 a war broke out between the northern states and eleven southern states of the United States. The southern states wished to form a country of their own. Slavery was one of the causes of the war. Most of the people of the South believed in slavery. Many of them owned slaves. Most of the people of the North were against slavery. There were not many slaves in the North.

Abraham Lincoln was the president of the United States when the war broke out. On September 22, 1862, he took a very important step. He proclaimed that on the next New Year's Day the slaves of the southern states were to be set free. The proclamation meant the freeing of about three million slaves. It is called the Emancipation Proclamation. (See CONFEDERATE STATES; LINCOLN, ABRAHAM.)

ENERGY "How much energy he has," we say when we see a little boy jumping up and down. "What a lot of energy that takes," we say when we see an expressman carrying a heavy trunk up a flight of steps. All work and play take energy. Energy is the ability to make things move.

Green plants make food for themselves. To do so they must have energy. They get it directly from the sun. As sunlight, which is one form of energy, shines on the plants, they are able to put water and carbon dioxide together to make sugar. People and all other animals get their energy from the sun, too, but secondhand. For they eat plants or animals that eat plants. Much of the food animals eat "burns" slowly in their bodies to produce muscular energy and heat, another form of energy.

Water rushing over a dam can turn a big water wheel. It has energy because it is moving fast. A stick of dynamite can blow up a building. It has what we call chemical energy. Electricity, magnetism, and sound are among the other forms of energy. We can use them all to make things move.

We are just beginning to harness still another form of energy—atomic energy. In time we may be using atomic energy to do most of the work of the world.

Energy is needed for work or play.

Hero's engine worked by jets of steam.

ENGINES, HEAT Much of the work of the world is done by heat engines. In these engines heat is used to make things move. There are heat engines of many kinds.

The oldest heat engine we know about was built nearly 2,100 years ago by a Greek named Hero. When a fire was built under the boiler, the water turned to steam. Steam takes up much more room than the water it comes from. In Hero's engine the steam forced itself up through a tube into a hollow ball. From there it forced its way out through two curved tubes. The jets of steam coming out kicked the tubes backward. As they moved backward they made the ball whirl around.

Hero had a wonderful idea. But people thought of his engine as only an interesting toy, and nothing came of it. It was not until about 1,800 years later that steam engines came into use. Then they were built on a different plan. The steam from a boiler forced its way into a cylinder. There it pushed against a movable disk called a piston. It moved the piston and whatever was attached to the piston. In the first usable steam engine the piston was attached to a long rod that worked a pump. This engine, which was built in 1698, was used to pump water out of a coal mine.

We call James Watt the inventor of the steam engine. He built the first steam engine that really worked well. His engine had a sliding valve. This sent the steam into the cylinder on first one side of the piston and then the other.

The steam engine in the locomotive pictured below is built on Watt's idea. The sliding valve can be seen above the piston. As the valve lets steam enter on one side of the piston, it lets steam escape from the other side. The "chuff-chuff" of a steam locomotive is the sound made as steam pushes the piston in first one direction and then in the other direction.

Steam engines like this once ran many kinds of machines besides locomotives—boats, farm machinery, steam shovels, pumps, pile drivers, and still others. Now steam turbines and other kinds of engines are used for most kinds of work.

STEAM LOCOMOTIVE

Boiler   Firebox

Piston

Steam turbines use the force of steam, too. But in turbines the steam pushes against many curved metal blades instead of pushing against a piston. The blades of a turbine are attached to a wheel which is mounted on a rod, or shaft. The wheel, together with its blades, is called a rotor. The rotor fits inside a heavy metal case. The steam strikes the rotor blades with such force that the rotor spins around very fast. As it spins it can be made to turn other wheels. Steam turbines are found in many powerhouses. They turn big generators that furnish electricity.

In steam engines and steam turbines the water is in a boiler. Fuel of some kind must be burned under the boiler to make the water turn to steam.

The engines in automobiles are heat engines, too. But there is a big difference between these engines and engines driven by steam. In an automobile engine the fuel—gasoline—burns inside the engine.

An automobile engine is made up of at least four cylinders. In each cylinder there is a piston that can move up and down. Each cylinder has an opening that can let in a mixture of air and fuel. There is also a spark plug, and an opening through which the burned gas can escape.

Air is needed for burning. The gasoline must change to a gas and it must be mixed with air before it goes into a cylinder. The mixing is done in the carburetor. As a gasoline engine runs, four strokes are repeated

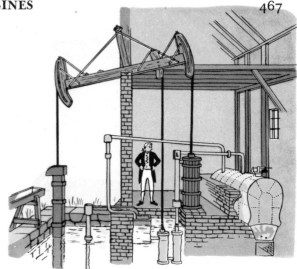

Watt's early steam engines were used to pump water out of coal mines.

in each cylinder over and over again. First the piston moves down and the mixture of gas and air comes in from the carburetor (stroke 1). The piston then moves up (stroke 2). It squeezes the mixture into a much smaller space. A spark then jumps across the gap in the spark plug and makes the gas explode. The explosion pushes the piston down (stroke 3). Then the piston moves up again, pushing out the waste gases (stroke 4). A rod from the piston is fastened to a crankshaft. The turning of the crankshaft is what makes the drive wheels of the car turn.

A car with only one cylinder would jump along like a jack rabbit. For only one of the four strokes of the piston is a power stroke —stroke 3. In a car engine the power stroke comes in one cylinder after another. Most automobile engines have either six or eight cylinders. Gasoline engines have been built with as many as 28 cylinders. But one-cylinder engines are useful for such work as pumping water on a farm.

Diesel engines have taken the place of steam engines in most trains and ships. They have taken the place of gasoline engines in many trucks. Diesel engines are much like gasoline engines, but they are simpler. And the fuel oil they use is cheaper than gasoline.

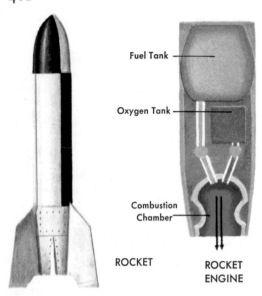

ROCKET   ROCKET
                ENGINE

Rockets can travel in outer space because they carry their own oxygen for burning with them. Usually this oxygen is in a compressed liquid form.

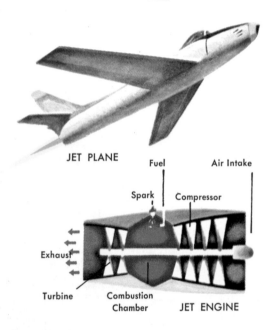

JET PLANE

JET ENGINE

Jet engines need a constant supply of air. The air is compressed and fed into the combustion chamber where it mixes with fuel. The burning of this mixture provides power.

A diesel engine has cylinders just as a gasoline engine has. But it does not have spark plugs or a carburetor. Air comes into the cylinder as the piston moves down. The piston moves up and squeezes the air into a small space. Compressing the air makes it very hot. Then a powerful pump squirts a little fuel oil into the cylinder. The air is so hot that the oil explodes and forces the piston down. The piston then moves up and forces out the waste gases.

A diesel engine is big and heavy. The walls of the cylinders must be very strong. For this reason, ordinary automobiles do not have diesel engines.

In many locomotives and ships with diesel engines the engines do not drive the locomotives and ships directly. Instead they turn generators. The generators furnish electricity for electric motors, which turn the wheels of the locomotive or the propellers of the ship.

After more than 2,000 years, inventors finally got back to Hero's old idea. They invented an engine that worked by shooting out a jet of material. But instead of shooting out jets of steam, modern jet engines shoot out very hot gas. It is easy to make a toy balloon act like a jet engine. If one blows up a toy balloon, holds it sideways, and then lets go of it, it will shoot forward. The air inside pushes outward. It can escape through the opening. It cannot escape at the opposite side. Its push there sends the balloon forward.

There are different kinds of jet engines. The picture shows a turbojet engine. In this engine there is a compressor that

AUTOMOBILE

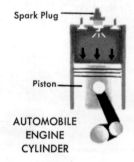

AUTOMOBILE
ENGINE
CYLINDER

Each cylinder in an automobile engine provides power only on every fourth stroke. Automobile engines usually have six or eight cylinders.

forces air into the combustion chamber. Fuel is sprayed into the chamber, too. A spark sets the mixture to burning. The hot gases escape, they hit the blades of a turbine and spin it around. The turbine keeps the compressor turning. Jet planes can go very fast. Some of them can easily travel faster than sound.

Rocket engines, like jet engines, move by shooting out hot gases. But rocket engines do not have to have air. They carry their oxygen with them. Oxygen is the part of the air needed for burning. Rocket engines can carry rockets hundreds of miles upward—up far beyond where planes can go. Rocket engines may some day make it possible to travel to the moon and to other places far out in space.

Now a new age in heat engines has begun. In all the heat engines up to very recent times some fuel had to be burned to furnish the heat. In 1954 an atomic submarine was built. In the same year an atomic power plant to furnish electricity for everyday use was opened. The heat comes from a reactor. Here atoms of ura-

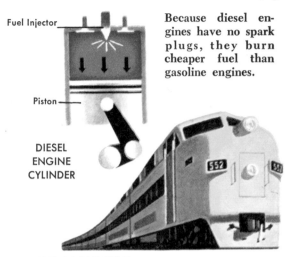

Because diesel engines have no spark plugs, they burn cheaper fuel than gasoline engines.

Fuel Injector

Piston

DIESEL ENGINE CYLINDER

DIESEL LOCOMOTIVE

nium change into atoms of other materials. As they do they give off an enormous amount of heat. This heat is used to change water to steam. The steam makes a steam turbine run. Engines run by atomic energy will make great changes in the world—especially in the parts of the world where there is no coal or oil. (See AIRPLANES; ATOMS; ENERGY; FUELS; LOCOMOTIVES; ROCKETS; SHIPS; SPACE TRAVEL; SUBMARINES; WHEELS.)

Modern atomic power stations have generators driven by steam turbines. Heat from an atomic reactor is used to make the steam.

England's villages are a link with the past.

ENGLAND Little England became a famous country long ago. It is in Great Britain, the largest island in the British Isles. The narrowest part of the sea between England and the mainland of Europe is the Strait of Dover. Living near Europe has helped the English people in many ways. And it is often said that an army of a million men could not have protected England from enemy armies better than the Strait of Dover did for centuries.

New England, a small part of the United States, was named for England. There are six states in New England. England is only about three-fourths as large as New England. But England has more than four times as many people as there are in the six New England states together.

More than 40 million people live in England. Most of these people live in cities. About a fifth of all of them live in London, its famous capital. London is a famous port and a very great manufacturing city, too. Only one city in the world is larger. In each of about 50 other English cities more than 100,000 people live, and England has many smaller cities.

No place in England is far from the sea. The little country has eastern, southern, and western coasts. It also has many good harbors easy to reach from any part of the country. West winds from the sea bring it rain and help to make English winters mild. Millions of fish live in the bordering seas. Even in early times, materials at hand were used in building ships. England's fisheries are famous. So are its big modern shipbuilding yards. In and near the port of Newcastle is one of the most famous shipbuilding districts in the world. It is on one of the country's great coal fields.

England's big steamers sail between its many big ports and lands near and far. They carry products of factories, farms, forests, and mines which English people need to buy or want to sell. Millions of people work at sea or in the ports to help carry on England's great trade.

Farm villages, some of them centuries old, stately country homes here and there, pastures in which cattle or sheep graze, orchards, gardens, patches of woodland, and well-kept fields of clover and wheat help to make the rolling countryside famous for its beauty. And from the farms much food comes. The English like beef, mutton, milk, and vegetables. But they need more food than their farms produce.

England's miners dig enough coal to supply fuel for its thousands of factories and to sell coal to other lands. But the English need to buy much food and many raw materials for their factories. To pay for them, they need to sell many products of their factories to other lands. Some world-famous English products are cotton cloth, woolen goods, china made in the pottery towns, cutlery and silverware made in Sheffield, and needles from Birmingham. Big steamers bring to Liverpool vast amounts of wheat for flour mills.

Among the things thousands of visitors go to see are splendid old cathedrals, charming villages, and great modern docks. In remarkable little England, they can see "twenty centuries in a day." (See BRITISH EMPIRE; BRITISH ISLES; GREAT BRITAIN; UNITED KINGDOM.)

Much of England's wealth comes from its factories.

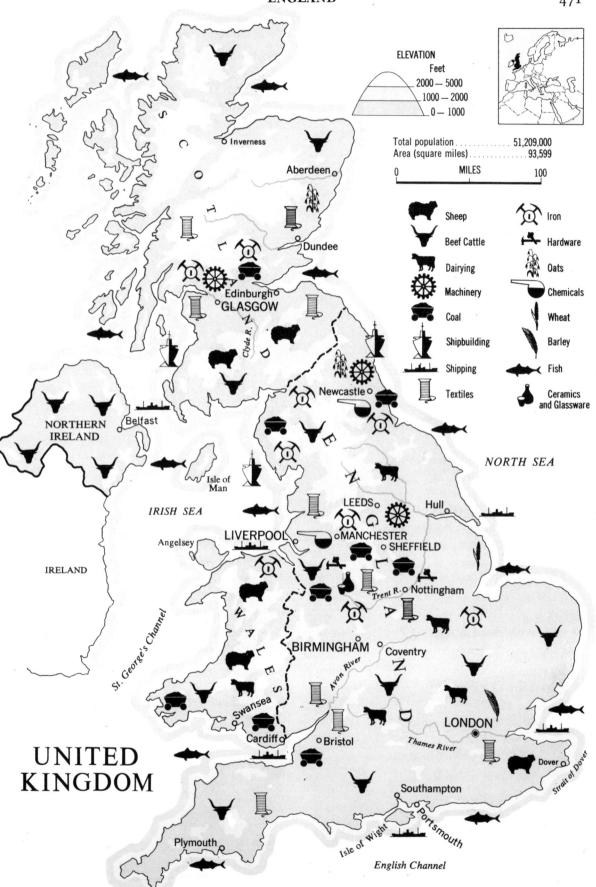

ELEVATION
Feet
2000 — 5000
1000 — 2000
0 — 1000

Total population 51,209,000
Area (square miles) 93,599

0   MILES   100

Sheep	Iron
Beef Cattle	Hardware
Dairying	Oats
Machinery	Chemicals
Coal	Wheat
Shipbuilding	Barley
Shipping	Fish
Textiles	Ceramics and Glassware

NORTH SEA

S C O T L A N D

Inverness

Aberdeen

Dundee

Edinburgh
GLASGOW

Clyde R.

E N G L A N D

Newcastle

Belfast

NORTHERN
IRELAND

Isle of
Man

IRISH SEA

LEEDS   Hull

IRELAND

LIVERPOOL
MANCHESTER
SHEFFIELD

Angelsey

Treni R.   Nottingham

W A L E S

BIRMINGHAM   Coventry

St. George's Channel

Avon River

Swansea

LONDON

Cardiff   Bristol

Thames River

UNITED
KINGDOM   Dover

Southampton   Strait of Dover

Plymouth   Isle of Wight   Portsmouth

English Channel

British Flag

British Seal

ENGLAND'S HISTORY About 2,000 years ago Julius Caesar and his Roman army invaded Britain. They met there a fierce, warlike people. After a few battles with the Britons, Caesar returned to Gaul, which is now France. He soon went back to Britain with a larger army, and forced the Britons to agree to pay him tribute. Caesar's invasion was not an actual conquest of Britain, however, because Caesar and his army did not stay.

Nearly a century later the Roman emperor Claudius actually conquered Britain and set up Roman rule there. For 400 years the Romans ruled the land. During that time they built towns and forts up and down and across the country. The people of the Roman towns had comforts not known again in Britain until modern times. Good roads connected the towns—roads like the famous ones that led to Rome itself.

In time the Roman Empire began to weaken. Rome itself was threatened by barbarians who were pouring into Italy. The Roman soldiers in Britain were called back to help protect Rome. They left expecting to return, but they never came back.

While the Roman soldiers were in Britain, they had protected the Britons from the warlike Picts and Scots to the north. The Britons themselves had forgotten much of their old skill in fighting.

After the Romans left Britain, the Britons were not able by themselves to keep the Picts and Scots from pushing southward. The Britons finally asked some of the German tribes who lived on the mainland of Europe to help them. Three of these tribes sent warriors. The three tribes were the Angles, the Saxons, and the Jutes.

Many of these newcomers who came to help the Britons liked Britain better than their own homeland. They began to take over portions of the land they had come to defend. More and more of their tribesmen came to join them. The Britons—who had feared the Picts and Scots—now found they had more to fear from their rescuers. The Britons gradually were pushed into the western parts of Britain, and the Angles, Saxons, and Jutes took over most of the country. The tribes of Jutes took the southeast corner, the Saxons the rest of the southern part, and the Angles the north and central parts of what is now England. "England" is short for "Angle Land."

Although the Angles gave their name to the country, the Saxons became more powerful than the Angles. Alfred the Great— one of the first of England's many famous rulers—was a Saxon.

The Angles, Saxons, and Jutes soon found that they had to protect themselves from new invaders. The Danes began making raids on England. Soon they had a foothold in the country. These Danes came from the Scandinavian lands that are now Norway and Denmark. They spoke a language much like that of the Angles, Saxons, and Jutes. Sometimes these Danes are called Norsemen, or Vikings. Before they were conquerors they were sea pirates. In their long, swift boats the Vikings went from their homeland not only to England, but also to France, Iceland, Greenland, and even to North America.

Alfred the Great won a big victory over the Danes in 878. After Alfred's death, however, the power of the Danes grew. In 1014, a Dane became king of England. He was the famous King Canute.

Before many years the kingship went back to the Saxons. But further trouble was brewing across the English Channel in Normandy, a part of France. William the Con-

Roman Invasion

Danish Raids

William the Conqueror

Spanish Armada

Elizabeth I

Admiral Blake

Victoria

Parliament Building

Elizabeth II

Battle of Dunkirk

Winston Churchill

queror, Duke of Normandy, laid claim to the English throne. In 1066 William and his army invaded England and fought the English in the famous Battle of Hastings. Harold, the English king, was killed in the battle, and his army was defeated. William was crowned king of England. Since that time England has never been invaded.

For a time, England and Normandy were joined. French nobles were given estates in England, and they went there to live. They and their descendants came to think of England as their home. Normandy finally came to be considered a province of England. But in 1204 the French king seized Normandy for France.

An event of great importance to the English nation occurred in 1215. In that year a band of nobles forced King John to put his seal on an agreement, or charter, called the Magna Carta. The Magna Carta is thought of as the cornerstone of free government in England.

As the years passed, England's trade increased and her cities grew. The kings of England gradually made themselves more and more powerful.

Most of the important events of the past 350 years in England are usually associated with certain rulers. These rulers, the dates and the important events of their reigns, are listed below:

HENRY VIII (1509-1547)

Henry VIII fought with the Roman Catholic Church when the pope refused to give him a divorce from the first of his six wives. The struggle led to the separation of the English Church from the Roman Catholic Church. On the continent of Europe, the Protestant Reformation was taking place, and many groups were breaking away from the Roman Catholic Church.

ELIZABETH I (1558-1603)

Elizabeth was a daughter of Henry VIII. During her reign the English navy defeated the Spanish Armada, and England became a leading sea power. British ships circled the world, and British traders set up posts in many lands. Some of England's greatest writers were also at work during this period. Shakespeare was one of them.

CHARLES I (1625-1649)

In 1642 a civil war broke out because Charles wanted to rule without Parliament. The Puritans controlled Parliament. Oliver Cromwell, their leader, took command of the government after Charles was beheaded in 1649. After Cromwell's death in 1658, his son succeeded him. In 1660 the country, weary of Cromwell rule, accepted Charles II as king. The years that Charles II ruled are often spoken of as the Restoration Period in England because the kings were restored to power. Their power, however, was limited by Parliament.

GEORGE III (1760-1820)

The harsh taxes imposed on the 13 American colonies by George III led to the Revolutionary War, which began in 1776. These colonies won their independence and became the United States of America. A war with France began in 1793 and lasted with only slight pauses until the defeat of Napoleon at Waterloo in 1815.

The invention of the steam engine in 1769 led to England's becoming an important industrial nation. Factories sprang up and cities grew rapidly as the Industrial Revolution gained force.

VICTORIA (1837-1901)

The British Empire reached its peak during the reign of Victoria. New Zealand, the Gold Coast, Nigeria, Cyprus, Hong Kong, and other territories were added to an Empire which already included India, Australia, Canada, Singapore, and other lands in every part of the world. In 1899 the Boer War began between England and Dutch settlers in South Africa. England won, and added still more land to her Empire.

ELIZABETH II (1952-   )

By the time of Elizabeth II, England had fought two world wars and had helped many of her old colonies become self-governing. Today, England pins its hopes for the future on increasing her trade.

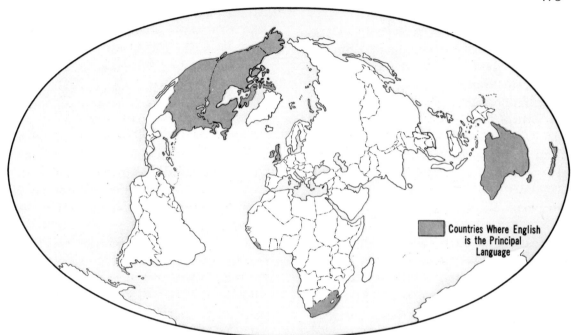

Countries Where English is the Principal Language

ENGLISH LANGUAGE Knowing England's history makes it much easier to understand how the English language came to be as it is. Many English words have come down to us from the language of the Angles and Saxons. We call their language Anglo-Saxon or Old English.

One might expect that the English language came from the Britons, the first people we know of who lived in England. All the four centuries the Romans were in Britain, the Britons kept their own language. But when the Angles and Saxons took over the land, they drove out many of the Britons. Those that were left were not strong enough to keep their language. They learned Anglo-Saxon.

The Britons that were driven into Ireland and Wales did keep their language. Later some of their words crept into English. But they did so long after the Angles and Saxons had come to Britain. "Basket," "cart," "shamrock," "plaid," "lad," "lass," and "cradle" are words from the language of the Britons.

Although many English words have come from Anglo-Saxon, it is hard for us to read Old English. It is almost as hard as

reading a foreign language. Words change as the years pass. "Seolfor," for example, was Old English for "silver," "praettig" for "pretty," and "maedgen" for "maiden." Besides, in Old English there are two letters that are not in today's English alphabet. They are called "wyn" and "thorn."

The Danes, or Norsemen, conquered the Anglo-Saxons and took over the rule of England from them for a time. But they were not interested in making the people of England speak their language. Wherever these ancient rovers went, they took over the customs of the people they conquered. The Danes in England learned to speak English. They did, however, leave traces of their stay in England. "Anger," "cake," "ill," "odd," "ugly," "sky," and "wrong" are some words we owe to the Norsemen.

After William the Conqueror defeated the Saxon king in 1066, French became the court language of England. The Normans did not drive the Anglo-Saxons out of England. They did not drive out the language of the Anglo-Saxons, either. For some 200 years French was the court language but English remained the language of the common people.

Then the English kings lost Normandy in France. They were no longer interested in keeping French customs. English came to be the court and fashionable language again. That English, however, was far from being pure Anglo-Saxon. Hundreds of French words had slipped into it. The Anglo-Saxons, for example, were not great traders and had no good words to use in trading. They borrowed from French such words as "cost," "price," and "expense." The new French words helped make the English of the years 1100-1500 so different from Old English that it is called Middle English.

Although many French words came into English, the framework stayed much the same. Most of the words in this Mother Goose rhyme, for instance, are Anglo-Saxon words. Only those that are in italics came into English from French.

Mary, Mary *quite contrary,*
How does your *garden* grow?
With silver bells and *cockle* shells,
And pretty maids all in a row.

French words that came into English did not crowd out Anglo-Saxon words that meant the same things. Instead, the Anglo-Saxon words and the French words were both used. We have, therefore, many pairs of words with the same meaning. The list below gives a few of them.

Anglo-Saxon	French	Anglo-Saxon	French
deed	act	proud	vain
harm	hurt	shape	form
kingly	royal	stream	river
pretty	beautiful	wan	pale

Of course, the many words which the Normans brought into the English language made it much richer. It is good to have more than one word for an idea.

Although there have been no conquerors to carry their languages to England in the past 400 years, new words have kept coming into English. Many of them have been brought into it by traders and travelers. These words come from all parts of the world. They tell stories of galleons sailing into the Spanish main, of trading caravans crossing the desert, and of adventures like those of Marco Polo. The list below gives a few of these word immigrants. It tells from what language they came.

umbrella—Italian	cocoa—Portuguese
skates—Dutch	potato—Spanish
tea—Chinese	taffeta—Persian
chintz—Hindustani	moccasin—American Indian
cigar—Spanish	tulip—Turkish

Some words came into English directly from the old Latin language. In the Middle Ages Latin was the language of the church and of the universities. Almost all the early printed books were in Latin. Latin words slipped into the common talk of the scholars and from there into the talk of the common people.

Some English words of today are manufactured words. The thousands of new inventions of modern times have made it necessary to invent words for them. The discoveries which scientists are making day by day make new words necessary, too.

One way of manufacturing new English words is to put together two or more older English words. "Skyscraper," "airship," "railroad," "manhole," "baseball," and "ball bearing" are words of this kind.

A great many new English words—especially new scientific words—have been made from Latin or Greek words instead of English ones. "Telephone," for instance, was made from the Greek words for "far away" and "talk." "Multimillionaire" was made from the Latin words for "many" and "thousands."

Sometimes Latin and Greek words are combined in making new English words. "Automobile" comes from a Greek word meaning "by itself" and a Latin word meaning "move." Some new English words are entirely made-up. "Rayon" is one of them.

Some new-made words are not called good English when they are first used. They are called slang. But many slang words come to be good English words.

During the centuries the English language has lost words, too. In the dictionary such words are marked "obsolete." Obsolete words may be called dead words. We meet many obsolete words in Shakespeare's plays and in such stories as those of King Arthur and his knights. "Quotha," "wold," and "yclept" are three obsolete words. They mean "indeed," "woods," and "called."

A living language like English is bound to change in more ways than one. Many new words come into it and many others are lost. The language has changed in other ways, too. The order of words in sentences, for instance, has changed. Verbs used to go at the end of the sentence as they still do in German. The verbs are simpler than they used to be. There are other such changes. Spelling has also changed.

Some people think that the language spoken in the United States should be called American instead of English. So many changes have been made in it, they say, that it is no longer English. Of course, it is not surprising that American English is different from the English of England. In both countries the language was bound to change, and the countries are 3,000 miles apart. Thus the English say "tube" for "subway," "petrol" for "gasoline," "let" for "rent," and so on. The English pronounce some words differently, too. But even though there are many differences between English English and American English, there are far more ways in which they are alike.

The nearly three billion people of the earth speak more than a thousand different languages. The language spoken by the most people is Chinese. Next comes English. English is the "mother tongue" of more than 265,000,000 people. Besides, many thousands of people speak English in addition to their own language. Trade and travel have carried English far and wide. Although it is not spoken by the most people, it has come closer to spreading over the whole earth than any other language. (See ANGLO-SAXONS; ENGLAND'S HISTORY; LANGUAGES; LATIN; NAMES; SLANG; VIKINGS; VOCABULARY; WILLIAM THE CONQUEROR.)

INFLUENCES ON THE ENGLISH LANGUAGE

Anglo-Saxon Settlement

Danish Invasion

Norman Conquest

Roman Invasion

Spanish Settlement

American Indian Cultures

Modern Communication

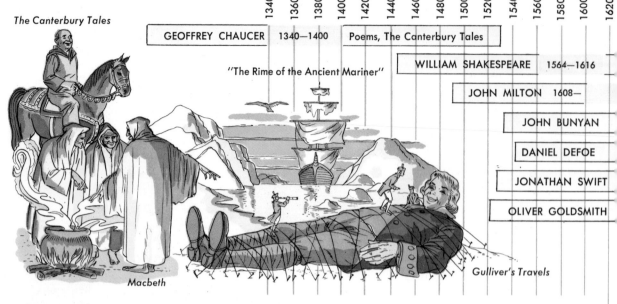

The Canterbury Tales

"The Rime of the Ancient Mariner"

Macbeth

Gulliver's Travels

	1340	1360	1380	1400	1420	1440	1460	1480	1500	1520	1540	1560	1580	1600	1620

GEOFFREY CHAUCER 1340—1400 Poems, The Canterbury Tales

WILLIAM SHAKESPEARE 1564—1616

JOHN MILTON 1608—

JOHN BUNYAN

DANIEL DEFOE

JONATHAN SWIFT

OLIVER GOLDSMITH

ENGLISH WRITERS *Beowulf* is a famous English poem. It is more than 1,000 years old. The poem is named for its hero, a mighty warrior. Beowulf, the poem tells, saved a Danish tribe by battling the monster Grendel and then diving deep into the sea to kill the mother of the monster. Beowulf in time became king of his tribe. He was killed in a fight with a dragon. The story is exciting, but not many people today can read it as it was written. For it was written in Old English, which is very different from the English of today.

No one knows who wrote *Beowulf*. But we do know of some great English writers who wrote in the days of Old English. Much of the writing in England in those days was done in monasteries. Caedmon (KAD mun) and Bede were two of the first great writers of England. Near the end of the seventh century Caedmon, in a monastery on the Yorkshire coast, told stories from the Bible in poetry. He wrote in Old English.

A little later Bede, in the monastery of Jarrow, wrote his *History of the English Church*. But Bede wrote, as did most church people, in Latin.

Chaucer is often called the father of English literature. He lived 700 years after Caedmon and Bede. He wrote in what we now call Middle English. Middle English is much more like the English of today than is Old English. Some of it, in fact, is rather easy to read. Here are two lines from Chaucer's famous *Canterbury Tales*:

"As lene was his horse as is a rake
And he was not right fat, I undertake."

There have been many great English writers from Chaucer's time on. The list below gives a few of them. Most of the writers in this list have written poems or stories which children as well as grownups enjoy. (See CARROLL, LEWIS; DEFOE, DANIEL; ENGLISH LANGUAGE; KIPLING, RUDYARD; SHAKESPEARE, WILLIAM; STEVENSON, ROBERT LOUIS.)

Through the Looking-Glass

Peter Pan

The Jungle Book

	1340	1360	1380	1400	1420	1440	1460	1480	1500	1520	1540	1560	1580	1600	1620

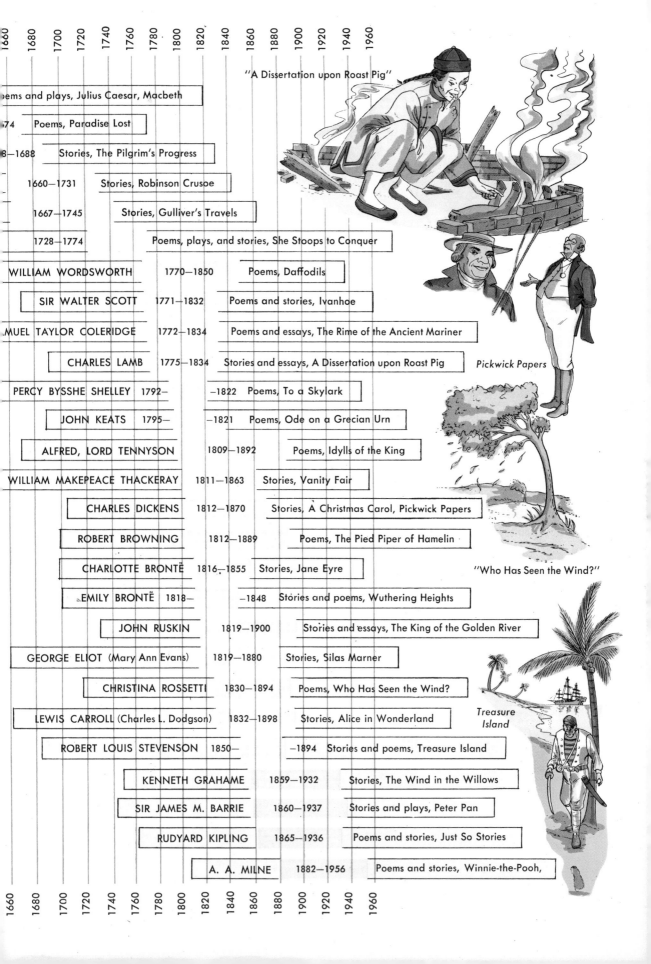

Timeline years across top: 1660 1680 1700 1720 1740 1760 1780 1800 1820 1840 1860 1880 1900 1920 1940 1960

"A Dissertation upon Roast Pig"

...ems and plays, Julius Caesar, Macbeth

...74   Poems, Paradise Lost

...8—1688   Stories, The Pilgrim's Progress

1660—1731   Stories, Robinson Crusoe

1667—1745   Stories, Gulliver's Travels

1728—1774   Poems, plays, and stories, She Stoops to Conquer

WILLIAM WORDSWORTH   1770—1850   Poems, Daffodils

SIR WALTER SCOTT   1771—1832   Poems and stories, Ivanhoe

...MUEL TAYLOR COLERIDGE   1772—1834   Poems and essays, The Rime of the Ancient Mariner

CHARLES LAMB   1775—1834   Stories and essays, A Dissertation upon Roast Pig

Pickwick Papers

PERCY BYSSHE SHELLEY   1792—   —1822   Poems, To a Skylark

JOHN KEATS   1795—   —1821   Poems, Ode on a Grecian Urn

ALFRED, LORD TENNYSON   1809—1892   Poems, Idylls of the King

WILLIAM MAKEPEACE THACKERAY   1811—1863   Stories, Vanity Fair

CHARLES DICKENS   1812—1870   Stories, A Christmas Carol, Pickwick Papers

ROBERT BROWNING   1812—1889   Poems, The Pied Piper of Hamelin

CHARLOTTE BRONTË   1816—1855   Stories, Jane Eyre

"Who Has Seen the Wind?"

EMILY BRONTË   1818—   —1848   Stories and poems, Wuthering Heights

JOHN RUSKIN   1819—1900   Stories and essays, The King of the Golden River

GEORGE ELIOT (Mary Ann Evans)   1819—1880   Stories, Silas Marner

CHRISTINA ROSSETTI   1830—1894   Poems, Who Has Seen the Wind?

LEWIS CARROLL (Charles L. Dodgson)   1832—1898   Stories, Alice in Wonderland

ROBERT LOUIS STEVENSON   1850—   —1894   Stories and poems, Treasure Island

Treasure Island

KENNETH GRAHAME   1859—1932   Stories, The Wind in the Willows

SIR JAMES M. BARRIE   1860—1937   Stories and plays, Peter Pan

RUDYARD KIPLING   1865—1936   Poems and stories, Just So Stories

A. A. MILNE   1882—1956   Poems and stories, Winnie-the-Pooh,

Timeline years across bottom: 1660 1680 1700 1720 1740 1760 1780 1800 1820 1840 1860 1880 1900 1920 1940 1960